DO NOT REMOVE
CARDS FROM POCKET

TITUS ANDRONICUS
& KING JOHN

A NOTE TO THE READER

These Notes present a clear discussion of the action and thought of the work under consideration and a concise interpretation of its artistic merits and its significance.

They are intended as a supplementary aid to serious students, freeing them from interminable and distracting note-taking in class. Students may then listen intelligently to what the instructor is saying, and to the class discussion, making selective notes, secure in the knowledge that they have a basic understanding of the work. The Notes are also helpful in preparing for an examination, eliminating the burden of trying to reread the full text under pressure and sorting through class notes to find that which is of central importance.

THESE NOTES ARE NOT A SUBSTITUTE FOR THE TEXT ITSELF OR FOR THE CLASSROOM DISCUSSION OF THE TEXT, AND STUDENTS WHO ATTEMPT TO USE THEM IN THIS WAY ARE DENYING THEMSELVES THE VERY EDUCATION THAT THEY ARE PRESUMABLY GIVING THEIR MOST VITAL YEARS TO ACHIEVE.

These critical evaluations have been prepared by experts who have had many years of experience in teaching the works or who have special knowledge of the texts. They are not, however, incontrovertible. No literary judgments are. There are many interpretations of any great work of literature, and even conflicting views have value for students and teachers, since the aim is not for students to accept unquestionably any one interpretation, but to make their own. The goal of education is not the unquestioning acceptance of any single interpretation, but the development of an individual's critical abilities.

The experience of millions of students over many years has shown that Notes such as these are a valuable educational tool and, properly used, can contribute materially to the great end of literature (to which, by the way, the teaching of literature is itself only a subsidiary)—that is, to the heightening of perception and awareness, the extending of sympathy, and the attainment of maturity by living, in Socrates' famous phrase, "the examined life."

TITUS ANDRONICUS
& KING JOHN

NOTES

including
- *Life of Shakespeare*
- *Introduction to Each Play*
- *Brief Synopsis of Each Play*
- *List of Characters in Each Play*
- *Critical Commentaries for Each Play*
- *Questions for Review*
- *Selected Bibliography*

by
Evelyn McLellan, Ph.D.
University of Nebraska

INCORPORATED

LINCOLN, NEBRASKA 68501

Editor

Gary Carey, M.A.
University of Colorado

Consulting Editor

James L. Roberts, Ph.D.
Department of English
University of Nebraska

ISBN 0-8220-1279-0
© Copyright 1983
by
C. K. Hillegass
All Rights Reserved
Printed in U.S.A.

Cliffs Notes, Inc.   Lincoln, Nebraska

CONTENTS

LIFE OF SHAKESPEARE

Many books have assembled facts, reasonable suppositions, traditions, and speculations concerning the life and career of William Shakespeare. Taken as a whole, these materials give a rather comprehensive picture of England's foremost dramatic poet. Tradition and sober supposition are not necessarily false because they lack proved bases for their existence. It is important, however, that persons interested in Shakespeare should distinguish between *facts* and *beliefs* about his life.

From one point of view, modern scholars are fortunate to know as much as they do about a man of middle-class origin who left a small English country town and embarked on a professional career in sixteenth-century London. From another point of view, they know surprisingly little about the writer who has continued to influence the English language and its drama and poetry for more than three hundred years. Sparse and scattered as these facts of his life are, they are sufficient to prove that a man from Stratford by the name of William Shakespeare wrote the major portion of the thirty-seven plays which scholars ascribe to him. The concise review which follows will concern itself with some of these records.

No one knows the exact date of William Shakespeare's birth. His baptism occurred on Wednesday, April 26, 1564. His father was John Shakespeare, tanner, glover, dealer in grain, and town official of Stratford; his mother, Mary, was the daughter of Robert Arden, a prosperous gentleman-farmer. The Shakespeares lived on Henley Street.

Under a bond dated November 28, 1582, William Shakespeare and Anne Hathaway entered into a marriage contract. The baptism of their eldest child, Susanna, took place in Stratford in May, 1583. One year and nine months later their twins, Hamnet and Judith, were christened in the same church. The parents named them for the poet's friends Hamnet and Judith Sadler.

Early in 1596, William Shakespeare, in his father's name, applied to the College of Heralds for a coat of arms. Although positive proof is lacking, there is reason to believe that the Heralds granted this request, for in 1599 Shakespeare again made application for the right to quarter his coat of arms with that of his mother. Entitled to her father's coat of arms, Mary had lost this privilege when she married John Shakespeare before he held the official status of gentleman.

In May of 1597, Shakespeare purchased New Place, the outstanding residential property in Stratford at that time. Since John Shakespeare had suffered financial reverses prior to this date, William must have achieved success for himself.

Court records show that in 1601 or 1602, William Shakespeare began rooming in the household of Christopher Mountjoy in London. Subsequent disputes between Shakespeare's landlord, Mountjoy, and his son-in-law, Stephen Belott, over Stephen's wedding settlement led to a series of legal actions, and in 1612 the court scribe recorded Shakespeare's deposition of testimony relating to the case.

In July, 1605, William Shakespeare paid four hundred and forty pounds for the lease of a large portion of the tithes on certain real estate in and near Stratford. This was an arrangement whereby Shakespeare purchased half the annual tithes, or taxes, on certain agricultural products from sections of land in and near Stratford. In addition to receiving approximately ten percent income on his investment, he almost doubled his capital. This was possibly the most important and successful investment of his lifetime, and it paid a steady income for many years.

Shakespeare is next mentioned when John Combe, a resident of Stratford, died on July 12, 1614. To his friend, Combe bequeathed the sum of five pounds. These records and similar ones are important, not because of their economic significance but because they prove the existence of a William Shakespeare in Stratford and in London during this period.

On March 25, 1616, William Shakespeare revised his last will and testament. He died on April 23 of the same year. His body lies within the chancel and before the altar of the Stratford church. A rather wry inscription is carved upon his tombstone:

> Good Friend, for Jesus' sake, forbear
> To dig the dust enclosed here;
> Blest be the man that spares these stones
> And curst be he that moves my bones.

The last direct descendant of William Shakespeare was his granddaughter, Elizabeth Hall, who died in 1670.

These are the most outstanding facts about Shakespeare the man, as apart from those about the dramatist and poet. Such pieces of information, scattered from 1564 through 1616, declare the existence of such a person, not as a writer or actor, but as a private citizen. It is illogical to think that anyone would or could have fabricated these details for the purpose of deceiving later generations.

In similar fashion, the evidence establishing William Shakespeare as the foremost playwright of his day is positive and persuasive. Robert Greene's *Groatsworth of Wit*, in which he attacked Shakespeare, a mere actor, for presuming to write plays in competition with Greene and his fellow playwrights, was entered in the *Stationers' Register* on September 20, 1592. In 1594 Shakespeare acted before Queen Elizabeth, and in 1594 and 1595 his name appeared as one of the shareholders of the Lord Chamberlain's Company. Francis Meres in his *Palladis Tamia* (1598) called Shakespeare "mellifluous and honytongued" and compared his comedies and tragedies with those of Plautus and Seneca in excellence.

Shakespeare's continued association with Burbage's company is equally definite. His name appears as one of the owners of the Globe in 1599. On May 19, 1603, he and his fellow actors received a patent from James I designating them as the King's Men and making them Grooms of the Chamber. Late in 1608 or early in 1609, Shakespeare and his colleagues purchased the Blackfriars Theatre and began using it as their winter location when weather made production at the Globe inconvenient.

Other specific allusions to Shakespeare, to his acting and his writing, occur in numerous places. Put together, they form irrefutable testimony that William Shakespeare of Stratford and London was the leader among Elizabethan playwrights.

One of the most impressive of all proofs of Shakespeare's authorship of his plays is the First Folio of 1623, with the dedicatory verse which appeared in it. John Heminge and Henry Condell, members of Shakespeare's own company, stated that they collected and issued the plays as a memorial to their fellow actor. Many contemporary poets contributed eulogies to Shakespeare; one of the best known of these poems is by Ben Jonson, a fellow actor and, later, a friendly rival. Jonson also criticized Shakespeare's dramatic work in *Timber: or, Discoveries* (1641).

Certainly there are many things about Shakespeare's genius and career which the most diligent scholars do not know and cannot explain, but the facts which do exist are sufficient to establish Shakespeare's identity as a man and his authorship of the thirty-seven plays which reputable critics acknowledge to be his.

TITUS ANDRONICUS

INTRODUCTION

This play can be classified as a revenge tragedy, one which William Shakespeare wrote at the earliest stages of his career as a playwright. The play was obviously influenced by both Senecan and revenge tragedies, even though it does not fully match all of the common qualifying factors of either classification.

Revenge tragedies were recent developments when Shakespeare was writing. Thomas Kyd's *The Spanish Tragedy* marks the beginning of the tradition. Characteristics of this tradition include and add to those of the older Senecan tradition of a "tragedy of blood." Both types traditionally end with a cartload of bodies and a stage drenched with blood.

Pure Senecan influences which are recognizable in *Titus Andronicus* include the following:

(a)   insistent, narrative moralizing
(b)   five-act structure
(c)   proclivity for sensationalism
(d)   action begins near the catastrophe, which limits plot complications
(e)   most action, especially violence, occurs off-stage
(f)   messengers report the off-stage action
(g)   the hero dies

Elizabethans, including Thomas Kyd, tried to shift from Seneca's models of declamation about outer conflict to an inner conflict of emotional and mental passions. Kyd was never good at this; Shakespeare too was poor at the technique until he developed a unique excellence in his mid- to late career. Then, the most elusive quality of inner conflict often proved to be sufficient motivation for revenge. Hamlet, for example, illustrates this as he vascillates while seeking some way to internalize his father's (the Ghost's) command to revenge his murder.

Although some divisions between Kyd's and Seneca's conventions seem forced, the components that can be extracted from *The Spanish Tragedy* must be regarded as influential because of that play's enormous popularity with Shakespeare's contemporaries. These characteristics include the following:

(a) a plot structured to build to a climax toward the end, with some use of suspense and counter-action
(b) madness of the hero
(c) inner motivation of the hero and major characters
(d) on-stage dramatization of some sensational action
(e) a villain whose excessive evil dramatizes the contra-Machiavel character, the popular Elizabethan interpretation of Machiavelli's *The Prince*.

Today, tragedy itself has become too large and complicated a genre to reduce to brief unarguable characteristics or definition. Its simplest definition is etymological – that is, *trages* (goat); *dit* (song). But some of the general conventions of tragedy that Shakespeare inherited are recognizable in *Titus*, conventions such as disguise, deception, intrigue, and a foreign setting (usually Italy).

What Shakespeare did not inherit in this genre were expert development of characterization, character conflict, and other essentials of general dramatic technique which we now regard as essential. Eventually, however, Shakespeare created memorable characters, and he developed and mastered uses of double themes with contrapuntal characters that still fascinate both audiences and critics. Furthermore, he learned to dramatize stories by structuring conflicts from which actions flow. But his dramatic skills, in general, are so poor in *Titus Andronicus* and the quality of poetry is often so sparse that critics have argued vigorously against his actual authorship of the play.

Nevertheless, enough evidence exists to attribute this play to a very new apprentice stage of Shakespeare's career – probably around 1596. Evidence examined to determine authorship includes internal evidence (the play itself), external evidence (documents about the play), quatros (single contemporary copies of plays), and folios (combined plays published after Shakespeare's death). Many critics argue that Shakespeare must, logically, be the playwright, based on combinations of that evidence.

Critics with positive points of view tend to regard *Titus* as an experimental development of the young playwright. Some dramatic experiments in *Titus* appear in later Shakespearean plays as master-ful accomplishments, such as the inexorable evil which forces the action to a climax; the pitting of two strong characters against one another in order to set up a complicated conflict (in *Titus*, Shakespeare's dramatic technique is already superior to his contemporaries'); the use of contrasting pairs of characters; the use of contrasting moralities; the creation of Aaron as a prototype of Iago; the dramatic, as well as the poetic, uses of imagery.

Sources for this play have also aroused some critical controversy. Shakespeare usually borrowed his story lines, but he seems to have used rather thin sources for this play. A probable source was a prose *History of Titus Andronicus*, which is believed to have existed at the time. Certainly, he did not rely on a favorite source, Plutarch's *Lives*, nor on any historical source, since no original Titus or Saturninus ever existed. He relied, instead, most heavily on the story of Philomela's rape in Ovid's *Metamorphoses*, Book VI. But he expanded noticeably from Philomela's mutilation (she lost only her tongue), and he added most of the characters and events when he wrote *Titus*.

As is true of all of Shakespeare's plays, *Titus Andronicus* is structured from conventions and traditions and philosophies which were well-known in Shakespeare's time; the play was not created in a vacuum, and although it is vulnerable to negative criticism, it contains some very good dramatic moments.

BRIEF SYNOPSIS

A grand procession opens the play. Gathering before the Capitol in Rome are the Tribunes and Senators, along with a crowd of citizens. Significantly, Saturninus and Bassianus, sons of the late Emperor of Rome, enter from opposite sides of the stage with separate groups of followers. Dominating the pomp and circumstance of flourishing trumpets and drums, Saturninus immediately tries to initiate a conflict. Appealing to his credentials as being the first-born son of the previous Emperor, he calls for armed support for his effort to succeed his father. Bassianus challenges him with a call for elections.

Marcus Andronicus enters with the crown and another expositional speech. After chiding the ambitious princes, he announces that his brother, Titus Andronicus, has already been elected as Rome's new Emperor. He then provides the citizens, and the audience, with the information that Titus has just returned from a victorious campaign against the Goths, capping a successful career of battle leadership, during which he sacrificed twenty-one of his twenty-five sons. Apparently persuaded by Marcus's speech, Saturninus and Bassianus dismiss their followers and pledge to end their quests for the crown.

Titus enters with a procession that includes his four remaining sons and a coffin. On display are a number of Goth prisoners, who include Tamora, Queen of the Goths, her three sons, and Aaron the Moor.

Titus inters his dead son or sons (there is one coffin but he refers to "these that I bring. . ."). One of his surviving sons, Lucius, then demands that the proudest of the Goth prisoners should be a just sacrifice for his dead brothers. Titus suggests Alarbus, Tamora's eldest son.

Tamora pleads with Titus to recognize that her son fought nobly for his country and that she loves him as much as he loves the sons whom he lost. She cautions Titus not to dishonor the family tomb with blood, and she directs him to imitate the gods by showing mercy rather than the power to end a life. Titus claims that he is appeasing his gods by severing and burning Alarbus's limbs; Tamora accuses him of cruel impiety. Alarbus never says a word. Demetrius urges his mother to remain strong and begin plotting revenge.

Meanwhile, Titus gives up the emperorship to Saturninus, and Saturninus, spurned by Lavinia (Titus's daughter), chooses Tamora as his bride. Here, Aaron's ambitions soar as he announces to us his intentions to reap the benefits of the high position of his mistress, Tamora. Immediately faced with a potential feud between Tamora's remaining sons, who each want to become Lavinia's lover, Aaron convinces them that they will best please their mother if they team up to rape and kill Lavinia instead of publicly squabbling in the Emperor's court. The boys eagerly join in this plot.

Their chance comes when the Andronicus family reunites with the new Emperor and his court at a hunt. Aaron selects a secluded part of the woods, tells Tamora to start a quarrel with Bassianus, then he leaves to go and fetch Chiron and Demetrius to reinforce her. In the name of revenge, Demetrius stabs Bassianus and throws his body into a previously dug pit. With their mother's fond blessing, Chiron and Demetrius then drag Lavinia off for their long-anticipated pleasure.

Aaron leads a drugged pair of Titus's sons, Martius and Quintus, to the edge of the pit. Martius falls in and Quintus tries to help him out, but he is pulled in just as Saturninus arrives. Before Saturninus can investigate that activity, however, Tamora gives him a letter that describes a plot to murder and bury Bassianus at this very spot. Aaron then produces a damning bag of gold which he had earlier hidden there. Saturninus declares that Martius and Quintus will be subjected to unique torture and execution, denying Titus's plea to allow bond and a trial. As they all leave the murder scene, Tamora falsely promises Titus that she will save his sons.

Chiron and Demetrius enter in high spirits with the raped and mutilated Lavinia. They failed to follow the orders of Aaron and their mother and, indeed, the plea of Lavinia, and murder her. Instead, they cut off her tongue and her hands in order to prevent her from naming her assaulters. The boys leave her there to be discovered by her shocked Uncle Marcus.

Titus, still unaware of Lavinia's desecration, totally debases himself as he pleads with the Judges and Senators to spare the lives of Martius and Quintus. He lies down in the path of the parade to the execution site, crying and begging. Lucius finds Titus, informs him that he is all alone, pleading to stones, then explains that he himself has been banished for trying to rescue his brothers. Titus assures his only remaining son that he couldn't be luckier than to live *anywhere* other than Rome.

Then Titus is once again appalled when his brother Marcus arrives to display the mutilated Lavinia. All four of them weep over the horrors which have decimated their family.

Aaron enters to perpetrate a particularly cruel hoax. He claims that Saturninus promised to stop the execution if one of them would send a severed hand to ransom Martius and Quintus. All the men volunteer, but Titus wins. Aaron helps him cut off his hand, then carries it off while glorifying the pleasure of evil for its own sake.

Titus appears quite mad already when a messenger delivers his hand back to him, along with the heads of his executed sons. Marcus finally rejects reason and succumbs to his own anger, and Titus, beyond tears, now pledges revenge. He orders the exiled Lucius to raise an army of Goths, then he himself organizes a grisly parade, with Marcus bearing one head, himself another in his remaining hand, and Lavinia carrying Titus's hand in her tongueless mouth. Lucius vows revenge as he leaves to raise a Goth army.

Later, at home, Titus vows to learn to understand Lavinia so that she can communicate. His tender mood, however, is shattered when Marcus kills a fly. Yet, Marcus finally convinces Titus that it is all right to murder *anything* which resembles black Aaron. Titus then wanders off to read with Lavinia and his only grandson, young Lucius.

Young Lucius's books provide the first means for the mutilated Lavinia to communicate, but she frightens the boy when she desperately begins plunging at his books. Then, when he drops them, she uses the stumps of her arms to select Ovid's *Metamorphoses*, and she turns to the tale of Philomel. This tale contains the clues of rape, treason, and murder in the woods. Marcus is then inspired to write in the sand by guiding his staff with his feet and mouth, thus inspiring Lavinia to do the same. Lavinia then identifies Chiron and Demetrius as the villains who mutilated her.

This information stirs Marcus to pledge the family to bloody revenge. Titus is ready, and young Lucius quickly catches the spirit. But Titus teaches the boy to avoid combatative confrontation and to resort to a subtle plot instead. The boy then delivers a message with a courteous mien while letting the audience know, through asides, that he is seething inside. Only Aaron recognizes that the "message" on the gift of "weapons" implies knowledge of the guilt of Chiron and Demetrius.

Meanwhile, Tamora gives birth to a black son, damning proof of her long affair with Aaron the Moor. Tamora sends the baby to Aaron with the request that he kill it. Chiron and Demetrius are shocked that Aaron has despoiled their mother. Demetrius wants to kill the baby, but Aaron protects his only son and declares that this issue of himself is more important than the mistress-mother. Furthermore, Aaron persuades Tamora's sons that they should protect their half-brother. Aaron enjoys an interlude of killing the three women who witnessed the black child's birth, and he plans now to deliver his son to the Goths for a safe upbringing.

Titus continues to project his reputation as a madman. This gives him the freedom to verbally attack Saturninus. Saturninus is fed up with the spoken and written libels which Titus has distributed throughout Rome. But Tamora dissuades him from killing the old hero long enough so that the cavalry, in the form of the Goth army, arrives in the nick of time and prevents the carrying out of the Emperor's orders to drag in Titus for execution. Saturninus is frightened by

Lucius's reappearance not only because of the army but because of Lucius's popularity with the Roman citizens. Tamora soothes her husband by promising to lure Lucius in for slaughter by deceiving old Titus with false promises.

Lucius exhorts the Goth troops to fight Rome because of the citizens' discontent with Saturninus and because of the wrongs dealt out to the Goths. A Goth appears with Aaron and his baby in tow. At first, Lucius wants to cruelly kill the infant while Aaron watches, but he is dissuaded by Aaron's plea for his son's life. Other than this impassioned dedication to his infant son, Aaron displays a complete, self-satisfying commitment to evil.

At this juncture, the plot to lure Lucius to Rome is initiated. Lucius accepts an invitation to attend a parley with Saturninus at Titus's home. Tamora, disguised as Revenge, with her two sons, disguised as Rape and Murder, call on Titus. Confident that Titus is crazy enough not to recognize them, they arrange for the parley to take place during a banquet at Titus's home. Titus persuades Chiron and Demetrius to stay with him, then he kills them and prepares to serve them in a meat pie to their mother during the banquet.

Lucius, Marcus, Saturninus, Tamora, Lavinia, and some assorted Goths and Romans are served by a solicitous Titus. Announcing that he is ending Lavinia's shame and pain, Titus kills her in front of his startled guests. When Saturninus learns that Chiron and Demetrius raped Lavinia, he orders them brought to him for punishment. Titus announces that they were baked in the pie, then he kills Tamora. Saturninus immediately stabs Titus and is, in turn, stabbed by Lucius. Other than the later proclamation that Aaron will starve to death while buried alive, this ends the multitude of dead bodies in this bloody revenge play.

Thus, the Roman empire is cleansed and can be ruled with justice again under the wise leadership of Lucius. Marcus and young Lucius also demonstrate the reappearance of mercy and wisdom. Marcus orates a general plea for the Romans to understand why Titus sought revenge, he presents Aaron's baby as proof of the dishonorable affair between Tamora and Aaron, and then he offers them a choice of electing Lucius as Emperor or demanding the deaths of the survivors of the Andronicus family. Lucius is elected Emperor by acclamation, and he dispenses a sentence to Aaron, then directs the disposition of the bodies. The innocent baby, it is implied, will live.

LIST OF CHARACTERS

Titus Andronicus

A popular Roman general who proves that he is not a wise statesman. Starting from a dramatic high point when he is proclaimed the new Emperor of Rome, he manages to alienate Saturninus, the Emperor whom he selects to replace him, in addition to the high-ranking Goth captives and, at one time or another, his entire family. After feigning madness long enough to gain a reputation for it, he descends to the level of a psychopathic killer. Other than mastering revenge, however, Titus learns nothing; therefore, he cannot be classified as a tragic hero.

Marcus Andronicus

The brother of Titus Andronicus; a Roman tribune. He represents statesmanship in contrast to his brother's warlike ways. Although he cannot save Titus or most of his nephews and his niece Lavinia, he does manage to help teach Titus's only surviving son, Lucius, and grandson, young Lucius, enough of wisdom and justice to leave the impression that Rome will improve under their leadership.

Saturninus

Son of the late Emperor of Rome and Titus's personal choice to replace himself as the new Emperor. Like Titus, he displays no ability to learn about statesmanship, wisdom, or justice. Arrogant and demanding in the opening scene, he remains so up to the moment of his death at Titus's bloody revenge banquet.

Tamora

The captive Queen of the Goths, she is Saturninus's rash choice for a bride only seconds after Lavinia is dragged away from his proposal. Tamora cavorts with Aaron, enjoys the high spirits of her sons when they want to rape Lavinia, and she provides consistently bad advice to her new husband. She dies by Titus's sword.

Aaron

A Moor attached to the party of captured Goths. Tamora, Queen of the Goths, is his mistress. A black Moor, like Othello, he is also a prototype of Iago. Evil, evil, evil—how he loves it. The mover of bloody action for most of the play, he is ultimately responsible for most of the thirteen dead bodies and for Lavinia's mutilation. Only the black son who is born to Tamora moves him to any recognizably "normal" actions. While fleeing to save the baby's life, he is captured by Lucius, who condemns him to a barbarously cruel death. Aaron regrets only that he has run out of time to enjoy more evil deeds.

Bassianus

The brother of Saturninus, he is a generally murky character. After a garbled opposition to his brother's plot to win the post of Emperor by force, he drops his own cause to support Titus. Just as quickly, he swings back to Saturninus at Titus's request. When Saturninus wants to marry Lavinia, Bassianus is granted his demand to marry Lavinia. When he briefly reappears as a happy bridegroom, he allows himself to be tricked into quarreling with Tamora. Demetrius, while supposedly defending his mother's honor, kills Bassianus with one quick knife thrust.

Lavinia

Apparently, Titus's only daughter. After her husband, Bassianus, is killed, she is raped and mutilated by Chiron and Demetrius. Once she is finally able to communicate what happened, however, she initiates the downfall of Saturninus. She is eventually killed by her father in order to free her from her pain and shame.

Lucius

The only son of Titus Andronicus who survives. At the end of the play, he becomes the new Emperor of Rome.

Quintus and Martius

Two more sons of Titus Andronicus. They are duped by Aaron and trapped in the pit which holds Bassianus's body. Saturninus orders them executed for that murder.

Mutius

Another son of Titus Andronicus. He is killed by Titus in the opening scene of the play.

Young Lucius

The young son of Lucius, grandson of Titus. Like his father, he not only survives, but he learns something during the course of the play.

Alarbus

The oldest son of Tamora. He is sacrificed to appease the souls of the slain Andronicus brothers.

Demetrius and Chiron

Two sons of Tamora; they rape and mutilate Lavinia. Titus's revenge is to kill them, bakc them in a meat pie, and serve them to their mother. That leaves the black bastard by Aaron as Tamora's only surviving son.

Publius

The son of Marcus Andronicus. He serves no significant role in the action.

Sempronius, Caius, and Valentine

Andronicus kinsmen who, like Publius, serve only minor background functions.

Aemilius

A noble Roman who steps in after the slaughter at the banquet scene to declare that Lucius is to be the new Emperor of Rome.

SUMMARIES AND COMMENTARIES

ACT I

Summary

This act consists of only one scene – the open area near the Capitol in Rome. Gathering to the sounds of drums and trumpets, the Tribunes and the Senators gather on a higher level in preparation for the proclamation of Rome's new Emperor. The conflict for this post is set when Saturninus, the eldest son of the previous Emperor of Rome, gathers his followers on one side of the stage and his brother, Bassianus, enters with his followers on the opposite side.

Saturninus appeals to both the "noble patricians" and his "countrymen" to take up arms and fight for his right to be Emperor. Bassianus calls on the people to fight also, but for the right of election.

Marcus Andronicus, the brother of Titus, enters with the crown in hand. He informs both princes that their ambitions have already been overruled by a special vote which resulted in the unanimous choice of Titus Andronicus as their next Emperor. Enumerating Titus's credentials, Marcus provides a brief history. Titus and his surviving sons have just returned from a ten-year campaign against the militantly strong Goth nation. Today's arrival marks the fifth time that Titus has returned victorious from long and bloody wars, faced with the sad task of burying more of his gallant sons.

Marcus then successfully appeals to the two princes to publicly withdraw their appeals and to dismiss their followers in honor of their government and Titus's heroic reputation. They both call off the proposed civil war and then withdraw to join the Senators and Tribunes.

With the triumphant entry of Titus and his entourage, the remaining major characters are brought into the action. Titus greets the crowd; he pleads for both honor and rewards for his four remaining sons, survivors of twenty-five.

As Titus prepares to inter the coffin in the Andronicus tomb, which is conveniently located within view of the Capitol, Lucius interrupts to demand a Goth prisoner as expiation for his brothers. When Titus selects Alarbus for the sacrifice, Tamora appeals to Titus's understanding of parental love and the nature of war. Titus responds that Tamora must understand that the sacrifice of her son is necessary for his deceased sons' souls to rest in the shadowy world of death. Demetrius advises his mother that she cannot save Alarbus but that she can begin a plan for revenge.

Lavinia arrives to welcome home her father and her remaining brothers and to mourn the dead. Titus expresses pleasure for her virtuous existence.

Marcus then steps forward to welcome them home and to inform Titus that he, Titus, has been elected Emperor of Rome. Titus immediately responds that he is too old, and he says further that in order to save everyone the trouble of electing a successor in a short time, that he would like an honorable retirement instead. Saturninus demands the empty post, and in anger, Bassianus vows to back Titus. Titus, surprisingly however, selects Saturninus. Marcus then leads the acclamation to accept him.

As proof of his gratitude, Saturninus honors the Andronicus family by requesting Lavinia as his bride and empress. But Bassianus demands that *his* betrothal to Lavinia be honored; the Andronicus sons back Bassianus and kidnap Lavinia. Titus kills his son Mutius, when he tries to stop his father from preventing Lavinia's escape, and Titus denounces all his children for their treasonous behavior.

Saturninus also denounces the family and chooses Tamora as his bride. Only Titus is not invited to join the wedding party. Fuming at the slight, he confronts his brother and his sons as they return to bury Mutius. Marcus has to convince Titus to allow Mutius in the family tomb.

Saturninus and Bassianus again enter from different doors, this time with their separate wedding parties. Saturninus threatens to punish his brother for the "rape" of Lavinia. Bassianus reiterates his right to marry his betrothed and then pleads Titus's case. Titus retorts that he does not want representation from the very man who caused his family's dishonor.

Tamora publicly entreats Saturninus to forgive Titus, then she privately cautions him against confronting the old soldier when so many of his supporters are gathered. She promises that she will find a way to "massacre them all" without risking insurrection. Tamora vows revenge against those who forced her to beg in vain for the life of Alarbus.

Tamora then fraudulently orchestrates reluctant reconciliation among all of the protesting parties. Saturninus voices forgiveness, invites Lavinia and her wedding party to join his own, and he accepts Titus's invitation to join a hunting party the following day.

Commentary

Act I presents a series of conflicts without focus. Without a sharp conflict, no plot exists; without focus, no drama exists. This problem, plus some weak characterization and a lot of poor verse, causes many critics to squirm about accepting *Titus Andronicus* as a play written by William Shakespeare.

Although these weaknesses must be acknowledged, they should not obliterate the innate talent of a young playwright who displays some dramatic strengths among the obvious weaknesses.

Conflicts in this act include Saturninus vs. Bassianus, Saturninus vs. Titus Andronicus, Tamora vs. the Andronicus family, honor vs. dishonor, and mercy vs. revenge. Where is the focus? Undoubtedly, during a performance of this play, the focus of the audience would dwell on Titus's stabbing of his son, because the sudden violence and blood would be shocking and memorable. If the actress cast as Tamora plays her part well, she will probably carry the act because she can work with the horror surrounding Alarbus's cruel death, and, in addition, she manipulates everyone into a fake reconciliation at the end of the act. Thus, she can be motivated by hate throughout most of the rest of the act.

In contrast, Saturninus and Titus vacillate throughout this act. They oppose each other, swear loyalty to each other, and then repeat the cycle. Marcus seems to be in a position of focus, but he loses it when he participates in the kidnapping of Lavinia.

Obviously, Titus is supposed to be the protagonist, and he will draw attention because of that. But the audience will see a strong man who cannot define honor, yet a man who storms into action—motivated by quickly changing interpretations of it. We know he fights. We suspect that he does not know what he wants nor does he think deeply. With those handicaps, he cannot initiate action as a good protagonist should.

Saturninus serves as a good example of a character who acts without discernible motivation. At the play's opening, he calls on his followers and the populace to "defend the justice of my cause with arms" rather than "wrong mine age with this indignity." Yet, the cause of persuasion is sufficient to sway him to "commit myself, my person, and the cause." As soon as Titus refuses the offer to become Emperor, Saturninus demands: "Patricians, draw your swords, and sheathe them not/ Till Saturninus be Rome's Emperor." Within moments after Titus orchestrates his election as Emperor, Saturninus promises to reward the Andronicus family and, for a start, he selects Lavinia as his Empress. When he is thwarted in that effort because his brother claims *his* right to Lavinia, Saturninus turns against Bassianus and the entire Andronicus family. With as much thought as he has given to all of his other actions, Saturninus suddenly chooses

Tamora, the captive Queen of the Goths, as his bride and the new Empress of Rome. Although he has not yet even been formally introduced to the woman, he accepts her advice on the proper handling of the Andronicus matter.

Thus, Act I ends on an improbable note. At this stage, we might well conclude that the central conflict will be between Titus and Saturninus, but we would be wrong. We might also believe that a classic revenge tragedy is developing, because so many characters mention *revenge*, but we would again be proven wrong by the actual development of the play.

ACT II

Summary

No change of scene or time occurs between the end of Act I and Aaron's soliloquy at the beginning of this act. With the wedding party just begun, Aaron is already reveling in lascivious fantasies about his affair with Tamora and his improved status as the lover of the Empress of Rome.

Tamora's two remaining sons, Chiron and Demetrius, interrupt Aaron's lusty reverie with their own warring lusts. They propose a duel to decide who is to win the right to seduce Lavinia. Aaron chastises them for carrying on this quarrel, especially when the Emperor will certainly hear of it and their mother will be dishonored. He further warns them that Bassianus is a prince who has the power to punish them for their very thoughts.

When asked how he proposes to have Lavinia, Demetrius responds that any woman, no matter the rank of her husband, can be seduced. Aaron takes a moment to smirk about cuckolding someone with the rank of Saturninus. But immediately after this aside, Aaron begins counseling the boys to be reconciled so that they may *both* enjoy Lavinia. He insists that Lavinia is too virtuous to be seduced, but he entices them with the thought of a lustful rape at the reconcilation hunt. Aaron further insists that they involve their mother's talent for treachery in the rape. Chiron and Demetrius, thrilled at the prospect, exit with their new mentor.

Marking the first change of scene, Titus enters to announce "The hunt is up." He cautions his sons to treat the Emperor well, primarily because his, Titus's, troubled sleep has left him with a vague foreboding.

The hunting party gathers amidst bawdy jokes about newlyweds and bragging about hunting prowess. Demetrius encapsulates the general tone with a thinly disguised threat to ravish Lavinia.

Setting the scene for the approaching multiple perfidies, Aaron enters to bury a bag of gold and hint at his carefully designed plot. Tamora approaches Aaron with lusty hints about what they could enjoy in this isolated spot. Aaron makes it clear that he wants nothing but revenge this morning.

With the approach of Bassianus and Lavinia, Aaron begins the plot anew with instructions to Tamora to start a quarrel. He exits to fetch her sons for a staged duel of honor. When pricked by Tamora, Bassianus and Lavinia both cast slurs about Tamora's affair with Aaron. When Demetrius enters, Tamora concocts a tale about a threat from Bassianus and Lavinia to tie her up and leave her to die of fright beside the viper-filled pit, embellishing the tale by reporting the truthful slur about her adulterous conduct, then demanding that Demetrius revenge the threat on his mother's life. No duel ensues; Demetrius merely stabs Bassianus, then Chiron finishes him off. When Lavinia challenges them to kill her too, Tamora wants to comply; Demetrius stops her, however, with the thought that revenge should include the loss of Lavinia's virtue. Tamora approves the plan but cautions the boys to kill Lavinia when they're through with their fun.

Lavinia pleads with Tamora to intervene, but Tamora reminds her that no one listened to *her* when she pleaded for Alarbus. Death would be preferable, declares Lavinia, and she asks that Tamora kill her. Tamora refuses to interfere with her sons' fun; the boys then throw Bassianus's body into the prepared pit and drag Lavinia away. Tamora waves them off, reminding them one more time to kill Lavinia when they're through.

Tamora declares satisfaction with Lavinia's plight but vows not to be happy until all of the Andronicus family are dead. She wanders off to find Aaron. She misses him, however, because he enters with Quintus and Martius, luring them on with the promise of a panther in the now-familiar pit. Both of Titus's sons complain about their foggy sight and wits, apparently in reference to being drugged. Martius falls into the pit, which is covered over with briars. Quintus notices fresh blood on the briars, so he asks Martius if he has been hurt. Only in the heart, replies Martius, by the sight of Bassianus's body. Aaron slips away, and Quintus is almost paralyzed by a vague fear. Demanding to know how Martius can identify Bassianus in such a dark pit, Quintus is told that Bassianus is wearing a ring that illuminates the hole. Quintus tries to help Martius out of the pit and vows to either accomplish his goal or join Martius. True to his word, Quintus falls in.

Saturninus enters just in time to catch sight of Quintus falling. Mistaking the fall for a leap, he goes over to investigate. At Saturninus's demand for identification, Martius replies that these two unhappy sons of Titus have discovered the body of Bassianus.

At first disbelieving, Saturninus is nudged by the timely entrance of Tamora to read a letter which contains a plot to murder Bassianus. Following the tip in the letter that a reward of gold will be waiting at the elder tree, Saturninus discovers the bag of gold that Aaron had planted there earlier. Tamora implicates Titus by reporting that he handed her the letter. True to form, Saturninus jumps to the conclusion that Quintus and Martius are guilty. He orders that they be tortured and executed without trial. Titus's pleas for bond and a trial go unheeded.

As the Emperor's party leaves with the prisoners, Tamora soothes Titus with the promise that she'll see to the safety of his sons. Titus urges Lucius to leave quietly with him.

Thus, no one is left at the scene when Chiron and Demetrius return with the ravished and mutilated Lavinia. After a few coarse remarks about their independent decision to leave Lavinia alive without hands or tongue to identify them, they leave her. Marcus discovers her and laments the loss of her sweet hands and tongue. He tenderly leads her away.

Commentary

At the opening of Act II, Aaron swings the focus onto himself and never relinquishes it again. Aaron's plot not only causes him to function as the protagonist; it structures a focus for this entire act. Therefore, at this point, the play tightens up after a meandering, confusing first act.

The conflict here clearly pits Aaron against the Andronicus family. Aaron's allies, Tamora and her sons, take action under her direction. In the only major departure from this turn of events, Chiron and Demetrius commit a fatal error when they ignore their mother's orders to kill Lavinia. (One should note that although Tamora utters the order in this act, Aaron first instructed them to do this in Act I.) In this particular act, you should also note that Saturninus, Titus, Lavinia, Bassianus, Martius and Quintus act only in response to Aaron's manipulation.

However, characterization is again weak. Aaron and Tamora speak often of a revenge motive, but they certainly do not move in classic fashion. What has Bassianus done to motivate revenge? His murder might be triggered because of his occasional vague mutterings against the Emperor, but this motivation is never strongly developed. Tamora is certainly supplied with a motive for revenge against the Andronicus family because they sacrificed Alarbus, but she has no right to defend her *virtue*. When she falls in with Demetrius's argument against allowing Lavinia to die virtuous, Tamora knows very well that she is guilty of adultery with Aaron and that the slurs by Bassianus and Lavinia do not justify revenge.

Saturninus's character is developing a consistency for rash action, but that hardly translates into an understandable motivation. He is still unaccountably influenced by the Goths in his court and, indeed, he never seems to have a trusted Roman adviser nearby.

Titus is a mere puppet in this act. He never initiates a strong action nor does he seem to have any internal motivation other than subservience to Saturninus.

Motivation for Chiron and Demetrius's rape of Lavinia is clear and their misdirected "revenge" is understandable. As for the sons of Titus, Martius and Quintus behave like sheep, and Lucius does not contribute a thing.

That leaves Aaron with the only strong motivation, and it is not revenge. He simply loves evil. He loves to plot, to manipulate, to kill or at least cause death. He detests every character thus far introduced and will never change his attitude about any of them. Although Aaron mentions ambition at the opening of this act, he is not really ambitious for anything but the opportunity to indulge in evil. However, his expressed willingness to betray trust is later upheld. This is evident in his contempt for both Tamora and Saturninus when he declares his intent "to mount aloft with thy imperial mistress,/ And mount her pitch whom thou in triumph long/ Hast prisoner held, fett'red in amourous chains." Aaron is identified as a contra-Machiavel character, which the Elizabethans distilled from Machiavelli's *The Prince*.

Contempt for virtue and honor is upheld as a prevailing theme during this act and will hold as a primary motivation for several characters as the play develops.

ACT III

Summary

Before this act is over, all the harm that Rome inflicts on the family of Titus Andronicus will have been done. As the act opens, however, Titus is frantically pleading with the authorities who are leading Martius and Quintus to their execution. Titus, a general who marshaled a grand procession at the beginning of the play, now debases himself by lying prone in the street in a feeble attempt to stop the execution march. Just as Tamora's pleas for Alarbus had been useless, so now are the pleas of Titus for his two doomed sons.

Lucius enters and tells Titus that he is alone, lamenting to the stones that make up the road. He also informs his father that he, Lucius, has been banished because of a vain attempt to rescue his brothers. Titus responds that Rome is "a wilderness of tigers" which is preying on his family, and that Lucius is fortunate to be banished.

At this juncture, Marcus leads Lavinia to Titus and Lucius. Whereas Lucius is speechless before the horror of Lavinia's mutilation, Titus is sturdy and has a lot to say. He expresses a grief that "disdaineth bounds," again curses Rome for what it has done to his family, and in a moment of foreshadowing, offers to cut off both his hands. Titus summarizes the wrongs perpetrated by the Romans that he had fought for: the execution of his two sons, the murder of Bassianus, the mutilation of Lavinia, and now, the banishment of Lucius.

Lavinia is crying; perhaps, Marcus speculates, because she knows that her two brothers are innocent of the murder of her husband. Titus begs to know what they can do to make Lavinia feel better: cut off their hands, bite off their tongues, plot revenge? Lucius tells Titus to stop crying, because Lavinia's sorrow increases with his. He then tenderly wipes away his sister's tears.

At this juncture, when horror and grief seem to have peaked for the Andronicus family, Aaron appears with a fiendish plan. He tells Lucius, Titus, and Marcus that if any one of them will sever a hand for him to deliver to Saturninus, then Martius and Quintus will be returned alive. Each of the Andronicus family offers to sacrifice his hand, and they finally concoct a team plan in which Marcus is to fetch the axe, Lucius is to wield it, and Titus is to contribute his hand. When Marcus and Lucius exit, however, Titus quickly convinces Aaron to chop off the hand. Aaron quickly complies, after promising in an aside to deceive Titus within the half hour.

Titus sends off his hand with Aaron in a spirit of hopefulness and service. He requests that Saturninus bury the faithful hand and return Titus's two sons. Titus regards the hand as a small price to pay for the lives of Martius and Quintus. Aaron promises Titus that his two sons shall soon be with him, and then he reveals in an aside that he means their *heads*.

Titus and Lavinia pose together, displaying their gore and horrible mutilations, while Titus expresses the immensity of his sorrow. Marcus calls for "reason to govern thy lament." Just as Titus finishes expressing the absence of reason in all that has befallen the Andronicus family, a messenger enters carrying the heads of Martius and Quintus, as well as the hand of Titus.

The messenger, a traditional bearer of bad news, reports that the sacrifice of the hand was mocked and that he feels more sorrow at delivering this message and viewing these events than at the death of his own father.

This sparks the first show of anger in the ever-reasonable Marcus. He urges the unnaturally quiet Titus to now express his overwhelming grief. Titus laughs, saying that all of his tears have been used up, and he declares that sorrow could only interfere with revenge. Urging his remaining family to vow revenge before the severed heads, Titus organizes a grisly parade with the remains of his family. He commands Marcus to carry one head, as he picks up another; he orders Lavinia to pick up his own severed hand with her teeth, and he sends Lucius off to raise an army of Goths. Lucius watches the pathetic parade exit, and then he vows to revenge the woes of the Andronicus family.

The final scene of the act is set at a banquet for those of the Andronicus family who remain in Rome. Here, Lucius's son, young Lucius, is introduced. Titus recites the family's woes for the morose group. Marcus reprimands his brother for suggesting that Lavinia commit suicide if she cannot stop crying. Titus cannot see the harm since she has no hands to enable her to commit such an act. He recites the sadness which he believes his daughter to be feeling, and he vows to learn to understand her so that she can communicate. Young Lucius suggests that his grandfather change the subject and try to amuse Lavinia; then he breaks down and cries.

Suddenly, Marcus violently strikes his plate with a knife. When Titus asks why, Marcus replies that he has killed a fly. Titus, outraged at the murder, commands Marcus to leave. He insists that the fly had a family, was happy and innocent, and deserved to live. But when Marcus compares the black fly to the black Moor, Titus closes the scene by joining in the violence upon the fly and then leading off Lavinia and Lucius for a story hour.

Commentary

Tension again eases at the opening of this act because Shakespeare presents no clear conflict. Titus and Lucius are reacting against both mute authority and offstage action.

Thus, when Aaron enters with his plot to trick Titus into severing his hand, he again swings the play's focus onto himself. After Aaron exits, this act sinks into meandering melodrama during which the Andronicus family is not even able to identify a definite focus for their planned revenge.

Both Titus and Lucius are vague about their quest for revenge. Titus seems to hear the two heads of his sons speaking, threatening no peace for their father "till all these mischiefs be returned again/ Even in their throats that hath committed them." But Titus names no names and describes no plans. Lucius is more explicit when he vows to "make proud Saturnine and his Empress/ Beg at the gates like Tarquin and his queen," but almost immediately he defuses this specificity by pledging to raise the army of Goths "to be revenged on Rome and Saturnine." Thus, we are left with the impression that the Andronicus family is pitted against all of Rome but that impression, like so many in the vague use of the revenge theme, would be an incorrect one.

Characterization remains weak or nonexistent for most of the characters, unless one supplies undue emphasis for the weeping capacity of the Andronicus family or the capacity for rage in Marcus. Lucius begins displaying leadership strength, but he does not actually do anything with it in this act.

The exception to characterization is, again, Aaron. He succinctly identifies his motivation when he declares: "Let fools do good, and fair men call for grace,/Aaron will have his soul black like his face."

When Titus writhes within the vision of the complete breakdown of nature, he irresistibly invites comparison with Lear's rage at the opening of Act III, Scene 2. But the difference in the quality of language illustrates why so many critics are reluctant to accept the two plays as being written by the same playwright. Lear challenges nature with "Blow, winds, and crack your cheeks. Rage. Blow." In contrast, Titus passively describes his grief in hyperbole: "If the winds rage, doth not the sea wax mad,/ Threat'ning the welkin with his big-swoll'n face?" And whereas Lear parallels the raging storm to "the tempest in my mind," Titus disintegrates to the distasteful: "For why my bowels cannot hide her woes,/ But like a drunkard must I vomit them."

The macabre, melodramatic scenes in Act III have aroused much ridicule. But a comparison to the popularity of modern horror movies should temper that contempt. Is there not something "modern" about displaying gory heads and hands, about severing a limb with a gush of blood, about overdramatizing death and mutilation? Perhaps comparing all this with our own bloody box-office movies can tap some understanding for the popularity of this play in its own day.

ACT IV

Summary

In a setting not clearly defined in the script, Act IV opens with a frightened young Lucius fleeing from his apparently mad, as well as mutilated, Aunt Lavinia. When the boy appeals to Titus and Marcus for help, they assure him that Lavinia means him no harm and urge him to guess what it is that she wants.

The boy reports that he had thrown down his books in his haste to escape but realizes now that his aunt loves him too much to harm him. Meanwhile, Lavinia is frantically working with Lucius's books, turning them over with the stumps of her arms. All three of them then try to guess why Lavinia is throwing the books into the air, and then, in the first breakthrough of communication, they realize that she is repeatedly throwing Ovid's *Metamorphoses*.

Titus reads the book at the page she has turned to and informs everyone that she has located the tale of Philomel which, he then deduces, identifies rape as the "root of thine annoy." Expanding on this myth, Titus realizes that the rape took place in the woods during that fatal hunt.

Searching now for the name of the rapist, Marcus is inspired to use his staff, guided by his feet and mouth, to write his name in the sand. He then hands the staff to Lavinia who uses her mouth and stumps to write the word "Stuprum" (rape) and the names of Chiron and Demetrius.

Marcus now joins the other Andronicus members in composing a litany of revenge, requesting Titus and young Lucius to join with him to swear that they will kill the "traitorous Goths," or die in the attempt.

Young Lucius readily learns the stance of revenge, and he cooperates with Titus's plan to carry weapons as gifts to Tamora's sons. Marcus asks the heavens to support this action of Titus and vows to do so himself as a welcome balm for the emotional scars which Titus has suffered.

In Scene 2, young Lucius meets Aaron, Chiron and Demetrius, again at an unidentified location, to present the gift of weapons. A model of courtesy and deportment during his presentation, young Lucius lets the audience know in asides that he well knows that he is dealing with villains.

Later, Demetrius discovers a message wrapped around the weapons. He recognizes it as a verse from Horace, but only Aaron understands that the Latin inscription translates into a recognition of the boys' guilt. He decides, however, in an aside, not to inform Tamora or the boys yet. During a brief exchange, Tamora's sons gloat over what they believe to be a successful humiliation of the Andronicus family and wish for somewhere between a thousand and twenty thousand other Roman women to enjoy as they enjoyed Lavinia. They all agree that Tamora would approve. Then the boys announce that they want to go off to pray for their mother, who is in labor.

At that moment, the Emperor's trumpets sound, announcing the birth of a son. The nurse arrives with the baby who is obviously Aaron's son since it is black. Tamora has sent instructions to have the baby killed. Chiron and Demetrius are shocked and angered at what Aaron has done to their mother. The boys realize that either the baby must die or their mother is ruined. Demetrius volunteers to kill the baby, but Aaron protects his infant son. He warns Tamora's sons that he will kill them if they threaten the baby's life; he instructs the nurse to inform Tamora that he will keep the son and he makes it clear that the child is more precious to him than Tamora is.

Chiron, Demetrius, and the Nurse all berate Aaron for planning to abandon Tamora and her family. Aaron curses them as cowards, making fun of their flushed pale skin while his black son exudes only calmness and smiles. Then Aaron reminds the boys that this baby is their brother.

Believing now that only Aaron can save them, the three frightened people turn to him for advice. As always, Aaron quickly concocts a plot. After learning from the Nurse how many witnesses there were to the birth, he kills her. He explains to the shocked boys that he will leave no witnesses. Aaron instructs them to go and persuade another Moor and his wife, who have a pale newborn, to give up their son in return for their promise that the baby will be raised as the Emperor's son. The boys leave with instructions to bury the Nurse, substitute the other baby, and then send the other witnesses of the birth to Aaron to be killed. Demetrius thanks Aaron for taking such good care of his mother. Aaron delivers his son to the safety of the Goths, who are to raise him as a military leader.

Scene 3 opens with Titus leading a group who bear arrows with letters at their tips. Titus instructs some to shoot the arrows into the air while Publius and Sempronius attempt to dig to the center of the earth in order to leave a message with Pluto. He identifies his motivation as the sorrows inflicted on him by Rome, and he assumes the guilt for aiding Saturninus to the throne.

Marcus and his son Publius cluck their tongues over Titus's madness, for they realize the need to carefully watch him day and night. Marcus also urges his kinsmen to revenge the loss of Titus's mind by joining the Goths in war against Rome.

Titus returns for a progress report on the trip to Hades. Publius reports that Pluto is ready to aid in revenge, but that "Justice" is unavailable. Titus is outraged by the delay and swears to hunt down "Justice" to perform her duty. He then lines up his archers to shoot their messages to all of the gods in a trajectory that will cause all the arrows to fall into the Emperor's court.

A clown enters with a basket and two pigeons. Titus calls for the messages from heaven that the birds must be carrying. The clown protests that he knows nothing of any messages from heaven and is only carrying the pigeons to the Emperor's court in order to settle a dispute. Titus convinces the poor clown to deliver a message to the Emperor.

Scene 4 features Saturninus and Tamora. Saturninus is carrying the arrows which were shot in the previous scene and is raving about the attacks by Titus. The old general's madness serves as no excuse to the enraged Emperor. Saturninus regards the appeals to the gods as libelous against Rome's machinery of justice and vows that if he lives, he'll order Titus executed.

Tamora soothes her husband's distemper but reveals in an aside that she is gloating both for her victory over the Andronicus family and for her escape from condemnation over a black baby's birth.

The hapless clown enters with Titus's letter. After reading the letter, Saturninus orders that the clown be hanged. He then orders that Titus be dragged in for execution, thinking that this will stop a subtle plot for Titus to become Emperor. But Titus is saved when Amelius dashes in with the news that Lucius has arrived with the army of Goths. Saturninus panics because Lucius is even more favored as an Emperor than is Titus. Saturninus is afraid that the citizens will revolt in order to advance Lucius to the throne.

Tamora reassures her husband by promising to enchant Titus in order to lure Lucius to his death. She sends him off to regain his good spirits, and he sends her off to initiate her plot.

Commentary

Act IV is largely a shambles because it is a repeat of the play's original problem with a lack of focus. Consider the action covered in this act: it includes the first communication by Lavinia; messages from Titus to Tamora's sons and lover which convey their guilts; vows and acts of revenge by Lucius, young Lucius, Marcus, Saturninus, Tamora, and Titus; and, of course, Aaron's plot to save his son. Groups move on and off stage to change the hodgepodge of scenes, always with some spoken reason but with dramatically flimsy motivation.

In spite of all the activity, only three major advances in the action are achieved: Lavinia identifies her attackers, Lucius arrives with the Goth army, and Tamora initiates the arrangements for the final, fatal banquet. Aaron's baby and Titus's madness occupy a lot of time without contributing much to the plot. Most of the characters bemoan what is happening but none of them grow in character nor contribute much to the action.

As usual, character development is difficult to discover. Although Titus is described as incompetent, his conduct will soon surface as a disguise. Young Lucius changes the most, because he learns the fundamentals of revenge. Aaron maintains his evil motivation, especially in his barbaric murder to cover up for the birth of his son.

ACT V

Summary

Lucius opens Act V with a peroration to the Goth troops, urging them to avenge Rome's recent victory over them. An unnamed Goth wants Tamora's death to be a part of the revenge. Another unnamed Goth enters with Aaron and his son in tow. He narrates the scene of discovery wherein Aaron had been trying to quiet the crying baby. Since Aaron chose to soothe his son with recriminations for being "tawny" instead of "coal-black," everyone realizes that the mother was fair.

Lucius quickly surmises that the mother is Tamora and stirs up the Goths with that news. In a rage because of Aaron's part in the cruel ruin of the Andronicus, Lucius wants to hang the infant where Aaron and the rest can observe its death throes. He orders Aaron to climb a ladder and hang the child.

Aaron suggests, instead, that Lucius save the child and bear it to Tamora in exchange for some vague, wondrous result. As an alternative, he can only conjure a curse. Lucius urges him to develop the plot; Aaron promises to reveal all the villainies if only the child is allowed to live. Aaron demands a vow from Lucius to protect the baby. Lucius asks what he can possibly swear by that Aaron would believe in. Aaron says it does not matter what he believes in, because he knows Lucius to be a religious and honorable man.

Having extracted the vow, Aaron reveals that the baby is his and Tamora's, that Tamora's sons killed Bassianus, and that Tamora's sons shared the rape and mutilation of Lavinia.

While Lucius raves at the villains, Aaron rather proudly admits to being their tutor but claims that their potential was inherited from their mother. Aaron presses on with his revelations of his involvement in the various treacheries. He shocks his listeners with the recall of his delight at the incident wherein he tricked Titus into sacrificing his hand in exchange for the heads of his two executed sons, embellishing his story with laughter until his tears run as fast as Titus's tears of sorrow; he recalls also being rewarded by Tamora's "twenty kisses" for such a successful attack on the old man.

When asked if he's sorry for anything that he has done, Aaron replies: "Ay, that I had not done a thousand more." He then recites a list of other cruelties that he has enjoyed in his lifetime and expands his desire to 10,000 other uninflicted cruelties.

Lucius decides that hanging is too easy a death for such a cruel man. When Aaron fantasizes about the pleasurable eternity of being a devil to torment them all in hell, Lucius orders him gagged.

Aemilius then enters to invite Lucius and the Goth princes to a parley at Titus's home. Saturninus offers any hostages which they might demand to feel assured of their safety. Lucius waves away the hostage offer with a request that Saturninus substitute pledges to Titus and Marcus, whereupon they all march off the stage.

That clears the stage for Tamora and her two sons to change the scene to Titus's house. They enter in disguise. Tamora decides that she will identify herself as Revenge when she knocks on Titus's door. At first, Titus refuses entrance to the trio on the grounds that they will interfere with his concentrated melancholy. But when Tamora hints that knowing who she is will change his mind, Titus declares that he is not mad and knows very well that she is Tamora. She declares, however, that she is Revenge, the enemy of Tamora, so she can help torment all those who have been cruel to him. Titus deceives her by pretending to believe the story, and he identifies her sons as Rape and Murder. He challenges her, therefore, to murder them and to bring back the heads of all other murderers so that he can pledge obedience to her. Tamora counters by claiming that her two attendants are actually her *ministers*, called Rape and Murder because they wreak vengeance on those guilty of the two crimes. After marveling at the resemblance of Rape and Murder to Tamora's two sons, Titus pretends to welcome them.

During a brief time when Titus absents himself from the scene, Tamora reveals her plot to her sons. She believes that Titus is both crazy and convinced of her identity as Revenge. This seems to present the possibility that she can invite Lucius and the Goth princes to a banquet so that she can split the alliance.

Titus returns to welcome them, and he makes a few more comments about their resemblance to Tamora and her sons; then he expresses the idle wish that they could also have a black devil Moor to carry out evil schemes. When asked for orders, Titus tells them to go out and find people who look just like themselves, because these people must be murdered for their crimes.

Tamora praises the plan but asks if it wouldn't be better to do that after Lucius attended a banquet, during which she would present the Emperor and his family for revenge. Immediately, Titus calls in Marcus and instructs him to deliver the invitation. Tamora then proposes to leave with her two ministers, but Titus persuades her to leave them if she does not want the invitation to Lucius to be canceled. The deceivers are deceived by their belief in Titus's madness, so they agree to the plan.

Titus then summons Publius, Caius, and Valentine. When Publius identifies Chiron and Demetrius, Titus corrects him by saying they are Rape and Murder and must, therefore, be bound and, if necessary, gagged. Chiron protests, but both are gagged and are unable to plead when Titus returns with a knife. Lavinia appears with a basin. Titus presents Lavinia to her tormentors, summarizes their crimes, and then details what is about to happen to them. He will cut their throats, Lavinia will catch their blood in the basin, then he will cut them up, grind their bones, bake their heads in a meat pie, and serve them to their mother at the banquet. Thus, he cuts their throats, catches the blood, and then they all leave, carrying the boys into the kitchen.

Lucius then enters with Marcus, Aaron and his baby, and the Goths. He tells Marcus that he is content to be there if Titus thinks it's right, but he wants Aaron safely held for testimony against Tamora since he does not trust the Emperor.

Trumpets announce Saturninus's arrival with his attendants. Verbal sparring between Lucius and Saturninus is quieted by Marcus, who calls for them to sit down to a peaceful banquet.

But Titus has other plans. After beginning to serve the banquet, he continues the flow of blood by killing Lavinia – to release her from her suffering, he tells the shocked guests. When Saturninus is informed of the guilt of Chiron and Demetrius, he orders them to be brought to him, but he is informed by Titus that they were served at the dinner and already "daintily fed upon" by their mother. Saturninus then stabs Titus, and Lucius stabs Saturninus.

Marcus immediately initiates arbitration by begging the Romans to listen to the truth that Lucius will share. Lucius then recites the wrongs inflicted upon the Andronicus family. Marcus picks up the story by displaying the son of Aaron and Tamora, then calls upon the Romans to decide whether the remainder of the Andronicus family should kill themselves. Aemilius calls for a vote to designate Lucius as the new Emperor. An acclamation vote accomplishes that.

Marcus summons Aaron to his punishment, then joins Lucius in a reverent farewell to Titus. Young Lucius is also pushed forward to kiss his grandfather a final time. At this juncture, Aaron is presented for judgment. Lucius calls for Aaron to be buried chest-deep and starved to death, portraying an end during which Aaron will be begging for sustenance. Aaron vows that he will not say a word; furthermore, he repents only any good deed that he *might* have performed by *mistake*. Lucius then issues orders for the disposal of the bodies, and the play ends with the mass exit of the survivors.

Commentary

Act V's bloody climax probably saves the performance. After the restlessness of Acts III and IV, the audience experiences a series of tense, shocking scenes.

The action climaxes in a blood bath in the name of revenge. However, Titus behaves like a pathological killer with his pig-sticking approach to killing Chiron and Demetrius in order to serve them in a cannibalistic pie at the banquet, not to mention summarily murdering his own daughter. The structural weakness of the plot then disintegrates into a morass of verbal maneuvering to put a rightful ruler in place, a situation soothing to Elizabethans but unappreciated today.

The weakness has been present since the beginning of the play; the two opposing forces which must be in conflict in order to create a plot are never clearly identified. In Act V, some of the conflicts are the Andronicus family vs. Saturninus, the Andronicus family vs. Tamora and sons, the Goths vs. Tamora, the Goths vs. the Romans, and Titus vs. Nature (madness).

Aaron is still pitted against the world at large but more as character motivation than plot action. He remains the strongest character to the very end, surely stealing the final scene from Lucius by manipulating his sentence to a horrible death into another show of strength. And, of course, he manages to save his son's life in spite of all the people who were determined to kill the infant.

Shakespeare provides Aaron with a total physical domination during Act V, Scene 1. While Lucius appears to dominate Aaron through capture and the planned executions of father and son, Aaron is perched on a ladder (thus physically dominating the stage) and is provided with shocking, single-action dialogue (thus verbally dominating the scene). One must conclude that Shakespeare favored this character from the beginning to end and probably should have written the play about him instead of Titus.

One other point of interest about Act V is the injection of the Morality Interlude. Since the disguise of Tamora and her sons were totally ineffective and the appearance of Revenge had little to do with advancing the plot, the scene is probably there as a result of the playwright's shrewd ability to give everybody in the audience something that they wanted to see. And the important thing to remember after all the negative comments about *Titus Andronicus* is that it was probably a popular play.

QUESTIONS FOR REVIEW

1. Comment on the effects of the failure of Titus to heed Tamora's pleas for the life of Alarbus.

2. How significant is the decision for Lavinia to marry Bassianus instead of Saturninus?

3. Why does Titus turn down the opportunity to become Emperor of Rome?

4. What is the consistent role of Marcus throughout the play?

5. Comment on Aaron's single exception to his life of evil.

6. Why are Martius and Quintus killed?

7. Why does Titus sacrifice his hand?

8. List five ways that Aaron contributes to the decimation of the Andronicus family.

9. How does Lucius convince the Goths to allow him to lead them in a war against the Romans?

10. How does Lavinia identify her rapists?

11. Comment on how Tamora uses her power as Empress of Rome.

12. Is there reason to believe that Titus is crazy?

13. Describe the effects of Act V on the government of Rome.

KING JOHN

INTRODUCTION

King John, like *Titus Andronicus*, is an early play of Shakespeare's. But unlike *Titus*, the greatest controversy about *John* involves the date of composition, not the authorship. So complicated is the controversy about the date that the only safe assumption we can make is that the play was written about 1590. Strong arguments support dates ranging from 1590 through 1598.

Besides its general classification as being one of Shakespeare's early plays, *King John* is specifically one of his early *history* plays. Because of his production of history plays over a span of fifteen years (1589-1604), Shakespeare is credited with the development of the history play as a separate genre of drama. All of Shakespeare's history plays were more concerned with arousing patriotic spirit than with adhering to historical accuracy.

Sources for *King John* probably did not adhere to historical accuracy either. But there is even more controversy about whether or not any sources were used at all and, if there were any, what they might be. A list of probable source material would include both *The Troublesome Reign of King John*, published in 1591, and Holinshed's *Chronicles*, one of Shakespeare's favorite sources. (Some critics think that the extreme length of *Troublesome Reign*, if Shakespeare did use this, accounts for *John*'s gradual weakening at the end; a hardworking, industrious Shakespeare simply grew too weary or too pressed for time to continue the dramatization near the play's end.) A list of possible sources would include John Foxe's *Actes and Monuments* as perhaps providing religious influence. And of possible interest to Shakespeare, one might note the *Wakefield Chronicle*, a Latin manuscript with some details of historical references which appear at times in the play.

But to comprehend *King John* properly, two of the most important views to explore are the Elizabethan concept of the order of the universe and the historical influence of the War of Roses. Even a slight acquaintance with these views can help with the understanding of some points of view in *King John*.

For a well-structured explanation of the order of the universe, see E. M. W. Tillyard's *The Elizabethan World Picture*. One image used to represent this view of order is the great Chain of Being. In this Chain, each link represents some thing in Creation. All things are linked, beginning with the foot of God's throne and ending with the humblest inanimate object. Together, they form a unity of the universe with an order which is determined by God. The top three links represent God, the angels and then man. But high as they are on the Chain, the angels and man are not intended to regulate or alter the order. Instead, the order of the heavens is supposed to be duplicated on earth. Part of this doctrine of noninterference decreed that a king, however poorly he might rule, should not be deposed unless he actually forced the breaking of at least one of God's commandments. This concept is a key to the actions and points of view of the characters in *King John*.

But this ordered structure of the universe has its exceptions. One method of accounting for these exceptions is that God granted the power of free will to angels and man. This free will can be used incorrectly to the detriment of the orderly maintenance of the universe. Another is that fate is conceived of as uncertain and is subject to disorders in the universe. The phenomena of these disorders is often represented by the wheel of fortune and horoscopes and activities of the stars. The turning wheel and the moving stars to some extent rule man's existence, with man frequently a helpless participant. But free will could challenge fortune, if either an angel or a man were willing to risk punishment by exercising it to challenge the universe's operation.

This orderly universe, however, was not the point of view of the Christian Humanists, who did not see morality as a black and white issue. Instead, they measured human behavior against an indistinct, gray standard of behavior. Within the context of this humanistic morality, where conduct was measured by the application of conscience, one should pay special attention to the Bastard's evaluation of his mother's illicit relationship with Richard the Lion-hearted. In that scene and in his general point of view, Shakespeare seemed to be more aligned with Christian Humanism than with any other philosophy. Most often, we do not find a total approval or disapproval of any character but, rather, a view that measures humanity against the lessons of conduct which are outlined in the *Elizabethan Homilies*.

While trying to understand the characters in *King John* by using either the idea of a strictly ordered universe or a fluid Christian Humanism, it is important to remember that, on the whole, Elizabethans showed an optimistic interest in all people, places, and things in contrast with both modern pessimism and medieval grim endurance.

Fears that may be linked to dissatisfaction with a disorderly universe, that certainly can be linked to the instability of a chaotic government explain the importance of the War of Roses to the comprehension of *King John*. The War of Roses encompassed about one century, during which England was agonized by a vicious civil war. Although the action of *King John* takes place prior to the actual War, the events are regarded as an early thirteenth-century indicator of the horrors to come.

The War of Roses involved the heirs and descendants of Edward III, who assumed the throne in 1327. It involved two opposing "houses" which are both traceable to sons of Edward III. The House of Lancaster (represented by a Red Rose) is linked to his third son, John of Gaunt, Duke of Lancaster. The House of York (represented by the White Rose) is traced through his fourth son, Edmund, Duke of York. Counting Richard II, a grandson of Edward III and legitimate heir to the throne, eleven members of the royal family alone were killed or murdered between 1400 and 1483. These ghastly, bloody years of intrigue and kingmaking ended when Henry Tudor, the last of the Lancasters, won a battle at Bosworth Field. Fighting against great odds, Henry defeated the larger, royal York army. Richard III was killed in this battle. Afterwards, Henry VII achieved an alliance with the House of York by marrying Elizabeth of York, thus finally reuniting the warring families.

Henry VII was barely royalty material, for he was the grandson of a commoner, Owen Tudor, who married Katharine of France, the widow of Henry V. But he was sufficiently politically skillful, and so he was able to hold his throne against all opposition. His son, Henry VIII, was the father of Elizabeth I, Queen of England, when Shakespeare wrote *King John*. So, Tudor sensitivity to legitimacy to the throne had to be protected, and Shakespeare, politically astute, knew this.

Also important to a conflict in *King John* is Henry VIII's struggle against the Church of Rome during his attempt to divorce Catherine of Aragon. Without accepting a king's sovereignty as superior to the Pope's, Queen Elizabeth would have to be regarded as an illegitimate offspring of Henry VIII.

With this Tudor heritage as part of Shakespeare's society, the contemporary attitude as to whether or not John deserves to lose his monarchy or his life, as well as our attitude toward John's usurpation of the throne, is not as important as his defective title. Thus, the Bastard's decision to remain loyal in order to try to correct the attitude of a wayward king is a correct decision for the time. Shakespeare carefully supports this point of view by rewarding all of English society who remain loyal to King John and loyal also to Prince Henry, John's son.

Historically, this Prince Henry became Henry III, who ruled prior to Edward III. Nevertheless, the point of view of the play clearly refers to the horrors of civil war which were learned during the War of Roses and were part of the lessons learned by the audiences of Shakespeare's time.

Altogether, the play mixes the historical accuracy with Elizabethan beliefs and does not pretend to be an accurate documentary of the reign of King John.

BRIEF SYNOPSIS

Appealing to the Elizabethan horror of war, this play opens with Chatillon, the ambassador from France, claiming England and all her territories in the name of Arthur, and threatening war as the only option. John stands firm as representative of England's right to remain a separate nation. He honorably orders an escort for Chatillon to carry his answer to Philip, King of France.

Eleanor, King John's mother, hisses that he might have thwarted the worldly ambitions of Constance (Arthur's mother) "with easy arguments of love," and she urges John to maintain the strength of his operative possession of rule—or else risk his relationship with her.

Suddenly a strange controversy occurs between Philip and Robert Faulconbridge. Philip implies that he and his brother Robert may not share the same paternal heritage. (He is referred to throughout the play as the Bastard). Eleanor chides the Bastard for shaming his mother. The Bastard corrects her by stating that is *Robert's* claim, unappealing to him (Philip) because if it's true, he is out of his inheritance.

However, the Bastard points out that his looks are much superior to Robert's, and he is, therefore, thankful that he does not look like old Sir Robert. Eleanor thinks, and John agrees, that the Bastard does indeed resemble her deceased son Richard, Richard the Lion-hearted.

Robert then presents facts which lead them all to conclude that the Bastard was, indeed, fathered by the former king. However, King John rules that old Sir Robert raised Philip as an heir, and that Sir Robert's will was too late in the chain of events to disinherit Philip.

Eleanor then intrigues the Bastard with the choice of remaining the heir of Faulconbridge or claiming his place as a bastard son in the royal family. Philip accepts her offer to become a member of the royal family, and he promises to fight in France. King John then renames Philip Sir Richard, and Philip arises as a spirited Plantagenet. (But he is still referred to as the Bastard throughout the remainder of the play.) Afterward, they all send Robert off to enjoy his inheritance, and Eleanor and King John hastily exit to pack for France.

Philip lingers to explore the social implications of his new identity, and Lady Faulconbridge interrupts him to demand the whereabouts of her son Robert, who has publicly besmirched her honor.

The Bastard frankly confronts his mother with his physical dissimilarity from her husband and requests the identity of his real father. After blustering about her honor and learning of the voluntary disinheritance, Lady Faulconbridge admits that King Richard Coeur-de-Lion was his father. The Bastard graciously supports her inability to resist a king's advances and thanks her for providing him with such a fine father. She then takes him off so that he can meet his new royal relatives.

The next scene is set in Angiers, during a conference with King Philip, Lewis the Dauphin, the Duke of Austria, Constance (Arthur's mother), and Arthur. Philip, Lewis, and the Duke of Austria declare their loyalty to the cause of the maturely gracious Arthur. Philip calls for battle in order to deliver Angiers to Arthur, but Constance cautions him to await the response of King John via Chatillon, who, coincidentally, arrives at that moment. The messenger brings bad news: not only did the negotiations fail but, due to winds which delayed him but sped the English ships, the British troops have already landed to fight against Arthur and his allies. Furthermore, these British soldiers are of "uncommon quality."

King Philip seems unsettled by this turn of events, but the Duke of Austria declares that they are ready for battle. King John enters then with a parley group to offer peace if Arthur's cause is retired. King Philip argues that peace can be effected only if the right to rule England is returned to the rightful heir – Arthur, the son of Geoffrey, John's older brother.

Constance and Eleanor enter the verbal battle. Eleanor declares that Arthur is a bastard, *not* Geoffrey's son. Constance retorts that Arthur is the image of Geoffrey, as could be expected of such a faithful wife as she.

The Bastard enters and adds to the blustering while King Philip tries to direct the parleying to a settlement on his terms. King John flatly rejects these terms, but he and Eleanor offer terms to Arthur which are similar to the ones which the Bastard accepted. Constance caustically rejects them, Arthur cries, and the conference disintegrates into a family squabble.

The citizens of Angiers are confronted for a pledge of loyalty "to England" from both the King of France, representing Arthur, and the King of England, representing himself. A citizen responds to the dilemma by declaring that they will pledge their loyalty to whoever proves to be *the* king but, until then, they will keep their gates barred. The two kings respond by ordering their armies to battle.

Messengers, and then the kings themselves, reappear to declare victory for the off-stage battle. The representative citizen of Angiers, unimpressed by the verbiage, keeps them locked out until they can produce a clear-cut victory.

The kings then agree to join forces long enough to destroy the arrogant citizen of Angiers. At this point, the Bastard realizes that he can maneuver the Austrians and the French into directing their fire at each other. Continuing the spirit of cooperation, a citizen of Angiers suggests a compromise – a marriage between Lewis the Dauphin (of France) and Lady Blanch (King John's niece). The union would give Angiers an option to surrender to the united families. All but the Bastard favor this solution.

Constance opens Act III in a fury at the betrayal of her cause. Frightened but proud, she refuses to obey the royal summons to appear before the new allies. They join for a conference on the day of the marriage, but Constance continues to oppose the new alliance, and the Bastard continues to bait the King of Austria.

Pandulph, the Pope's legate, arrives to demand that King John allow the Roman Catholic authority to prevail in England, and King Philip is shocked by England's *absolute denial* of the Pope's authority. Therefore, upon threat of excommunication, he withdraws from the alliance with England. Lewis, meanwhile, urges war in spite of the pleas of Blanch (King John's niece) not to betray his ties to her and her family.

Dramatizing England's initial success in battle, the Bastard displays the head of the Duke of Austria. King John enters to deliver Arthur to the care of Hubert and to deliver instructions to the Bastard to return to England to obtain war funds from Church coffers. In spite of assurances of love and protection to Arthur, King John later commands Hubert to kill the boy.

King Philip, meanwhile, bemoans England's victories. He is assailed by Pandulph's assurances of heavenly rewards and Constance's hysterical grief over the loss of Arthur. After Philip follows Constance to prevent possible suicide, Lewis expresses his own despondency to Pandulph. Pandulph "predicts" that if Lewis is ready at the proper time, the English will revolt when King John kills Arthur; thus, Lewis can claim the throne because of his marriage to Blanch.

Reluctantly carrying out his order from King John, Hubert makes the arrangements for blinding and killing Arthur. But Pandulph's prediction and King John's command are displaced by young Arthur's appeals to Hubert, who decides to hide and protect the boy.

Meanwhile, King John perches precariously on his reclaimed throne. Pembroke urges the release of Arthur and expresses his fear that Hubert has killed the boy. When his fears are confirmed by King John, he and Salisbury are both fearful about the consequences, and their fears unsettle the king. He is further shocked by the news that a large French army has landed and that his mother is dead. Thus, in a panic, John dispatches the Bastard to lure Bigot and Salisbury back for a chance to regain their loyalty.

King John then castigates Hubert for carrying out the order to kill Arthur. Hubert retorts that he disobeyed the order, and that Arthur is alive. The king apologizes.

Arthur, however, tries to escape and kills himself when he leaps from a tower. The Bastard, Salisbury, Bigot, and Pembroke discover the body, thus shattering King John's hope to reclaim their loyalty. When Hubert shows up to fetch Arthur, he has to defend himself against Salisbury's attack.

Salisbury, Bigot, and Pembroke defect to the Dauphin's invasion force, and the Bastard and Hubert are left to carry Arthur away and to try to resolve the problems he created with his impetuous leap.

The final act opens with King John submitting to the Pope's authority. Pandulph then promises to end the conflict which he, Pandulph, began. All of John's potential support has joined the Dauphin and, with Arthur dead, John has no choice if he wants to remain King of England.

Lewis flatly refuses Pandulph's order to end the hostilities. He also refuses the Bastard's rhetorical ploys to avoid battle. Just when the English cause looks bleakest, because King John is extremely ill and battles are being lost, news of the sinking of the Dauphin's supply ships injects hope. King John withdraws to recuperate at Swinstead Abbey.

In the next scene, Salisbury, Pembroke, and Bigot share their doubts about a possible victory against the Bastard's effective defense. The dying Count Melun unburdens his soul by struggling to them and informing them that many of the rebellious English nobility have re-pledged their loyalty to England. Motivated by Melun's information and advice, the three rebels exit to provide Melun with a quiet place to die and a place where they can save their own necks.

Bad news prevails in the next few scenes. Lewis, weary from a near-victory in that day's battle, learns about the loss of his supplies and the loss of English allies. Hubert bears the English bad news to the Bastard: King John has been poisoned by a monk.

In the end, England prevails. Lewis is ready to negotiate peace, King John is dying, and the heir-apparent, Prince Henry, gratefully receives pledges of unity and loyalty for the greater good of a united, independent England.

LIST OF CHARACTERS

King John

King of England because of his mother's maneuvering after the death of her elder son, Geoffrey. His claim to the throne, and thus

England's security, is vulnerable. His two best characteristics in the play are his loyalty to England and his defiance of the Pope.

Prince Henry

The son of King John, heir-apparent to the throne if his father successfully defends their line of succession. His only role in the play is as a unifying factor at the end.

Arthur

Duke of Britain, nephew of King John. As the son of the previous king, he is the natural successor to the throne. As long as he is alive, he is a tempting rallying cause for civil war.

The Earl of Pembroke, The Earl of Salisbury and The Lord Bigot

Three powerful members of English nobility who waver from loyalty to King John, to rebels after Arthur's death, to loyalty to Prince Henry.

The Earl of Essex

A member of King John's court.

Hubert de Burgh

A trusted henchman of King John. He remains loyal to all orders of the king – except for the blinding and killing of Arthur.

Philip the Bastard

Raised as the elder son of Sir Robert Faulconbridge, he accepts the conclusion that he is actually the illegitimate son of the deceased King Richard Coeur-de-Lion and then assumes an important role as a member of the ruling family.

Robert Faulconbridge

Apparently, the only son of Sir Robert Faulconbridge.

James Gurney

A servant to Lady Faulconbridge.

Peter of Pomfret

A minor character who plays the role of a prophet.

Philip

The King of France. He first supports Arthur against King John, then interjects religion into the controversy and abandons Arthur's cause.

Lewis

The Dauphin of France, son of Philip. He marries Blanch, niece of King John, apparently achieving a union between France and England. But he becomes the aggressor in a war against England when he is encouraged by Pandulph to take advantage of the weakness caused by King John's errors in judgment in controversies with the Pope and with Arthur.

Lymoges

The Duke of Austria. When the play begins, he is an ally of France, in support of Arthur's cause. He is defeated and beheaded by the Bastard.

Cardinal Pandulph

The legate of the Pope. He destroys Arthur's cause by instigating the religious war. Eventually, he helps arbitrate a peace between England and France after France's forces are defeated in England.

Melun

A French lord who helps to convince rebel English lords to save their necks by abandoning their brief alliance with Lewis the Dauphin against King John.

Chatillon

A French ambassador. He tries to negotiate King John's surrender to Arthur's allies at the opening of the play.

Queen Eleanor

Mother of King John and the deceased Richard and Geoffrey. She uses her son John to continue her role as the power behind the throne.

Constance

Arthur's ambitious mother.

Blanch of Spain

Eleanor's niece. Because of her agreement to marry Lewis the Dauphin, she briefly serves an important role in an alliance between France and England.

Lady Faulconbridge

Mother of Robert Faulconbridge and Philip the Bastard.

SUMMARIES AND COMMENTARIES

ACT I

Summary

Chatillon opens the action by beating diplomatic war drums. Speaking for the King of France, who is acting on behalf of Arthur Plantagenet, he claims England and other specific territories. If John refuses to willingly relinquish his title to Arthur, France is prepared to enforce Arthur's rights through war.

King John listens to the entire presentation, then responds that he is ready for war. He then provides Chatillon with safe passage but warns him that he must hurry to warn King Philip before England's attack.

Eleanor scolds her son for not heeding her warnings about the ambitions of Constance, Arthur's mother. When John blusters that the throne is his because of the power of both possession and right, his mother admits that he possesses it, but that he possesses it by power *only*—he did not rightfully inherit the throne of England.

Essex interrupts their conversation and says that he would like to introduce the Faulconbridge brothers. King John barely has time to decide to levy expenses against the Church (to pay for war expenses) before he patiently agrees to attend to the controversy about the Faulconbridge inheritance.

Philip introduces himself as the eldest son of Sir Robert Faulconbridge, a soldier who was knighted by the Coeur-de-Lion. Robert introduces himself as the son and heir of Sir Robert Faulconbridge.

King John questions the authenticity of the mixed claims to being heir to the Faulconbridge title. The major question raised by Robert is whether or not his father is also Philip's. Technically, King John rules that Philip is the heir because old Sir Robert raised him as a son, thus legitimatizing Philip; the evidence, however, indicates that Philip is illegitimate, a "fault lies on the hazards of all husbands." The claim that Robert, on his death bed, dispossessed Philip as illegitimate falls too late in the chain of events, according to John.

However, concerning the evidence that Richard Coeur-de-Lion visited Lady Faulconbridge while old Sir Robert was out of the country on court business and that Philip unquestionably resembles Richard, King John determines that Philip is probably his own illegitimate nephew. Eleanor then offers the Bastard the opportunity to claim his rights as a son of Coeur-de-Lion. When the Bastard declares that offer is better than his decision to insist that he belong to the inferior Faulconbridge line, Eleanor praises his attitude and urges him to join the English cause against the French campaign.

Philip then renounces his claim to the Faulconbridge fortune and assumes his place as an illegitimate son of Coeur-de-Lion. King John presides at a hasty ceremony for the purpose of re-naming Philip as Sir Richard. The new Sir Richard enthusiastically embraces his identity as a Plantagenet; however, he is referred to throughout the play as the Bastard.

As the Bastard is savoring and adjusting to his new social status, his mother bursts in to demand an explanation for the public shame foisted upon her by her two sons. The Bastard convinces her to name his real father who is, indeed, Richard Coeur-de-Lion. He assures her that she should not be blamed for succumbing to seduction by a king, and he thanks her for providing so fine a father. He then escorts his mother to meet his new relatives while assuring her that no one could behold his fine physique and declare her act a sin—without risking being killed by the Bastard.

Commentary

Conflict dominates this play from its opening lines. When Chatillon challenges King John in the name of King Philip, he introduces a number of conflicts: national unity vs. civil war, English sovereignty vs. the Church of Rome, York vs. Lancaster, stability vs. ambition, and world order vs. chaos. Unfortunately, the conflicts are not carefully controlled, and so a central weakness of the play must be identified as Shakespeare's failure to establish a dominant conflict with clever counterpointing of subplots. A component of *all* the conflicts which develop through characterization, however, is honor. Characterizations of honor include esteem and respect, good reputation, integrity, purity, and social courtesy.

For instance, when John's honor as a rightful king is challenged, his next scene involves an honorable resolution of the Faulconbridge dispute. He patiently unravels the legal and moral implications to reach a measured verdict in the dispute that, in itself, involves reputation, integrity and the purity of Lady Faulconbridge. This scene is followed by the Bastard's soliloquy regarding the social courtesies which are attached to his new station in life. This sequence on honor ends with Lady Faulconbridge's outrage about the attacks on *her* honor.

Before this act ends, King John's character has been established as a patriotic king who is conscientious about his responsibilities. But *his* flaw has also been established; he maintains a willful hold on the crown in spite of the *legitimate* claim of Arthur.

The Bastard is emerging early in the play as a strong individualist. His sense of honor and patriotism are just beginning to manifest themselves as he tests the meaning of his relationship to the royal family. He does not cling to his Faulconbridge ties when he is given the opportunity to claim his rights as a royal bastard. Nor does he castigate his mother for her illicit liaison with the king but, instead, he chooses to reinforce her sense of honor.

ACT II

Summary

King Philip takes charge of introducing the allies who have gathered just outside the gates of Angiers. He explains to Arthur that the Duke of Austria has volunteered to support Arthur's cause in order to make amends for killing Richard the Lion-hearted, Arthur's late uncle. Since this death allowed King John's usurpation of the English throne, King Philip explains that the Duke of Austria feels obligated to aid the correct realignment of Richard's posterity.

Arthur extends an innocent, loving welcome and graciously declares that God will forgive his uncle's death in return for Austria's defense of the rights of the young Coeur-de-Lion who has been wronged by John. Austria vows that he will not return home until Arthur is established with his rightful powers. Constance joins in the thanks and implies a more substantial reward once Arthur is king. Austria then aligns the cause with heavenly peace and justified war.

King Philip wants to attack Angiers immediately in order to initiate Arthur's territorial claims, but Constance wants to wait for Chatillon in case King John has peacefully relinquished the throne. She wants no unnecessary bloodshed.

Just as Constance finishes her request, Chatillon enters with the advice to forego the siege of Angiers in order to prepare for an attack from England. He explains that adverse winds delayed his passage but that those same winds speeded up the English army's advance, so an attack by a strong English army is imminent. Finally, Chatillon describes the royal English party as consisting of King John, the Queen Mother (whom he implies acts as an inciter of vengeance), Lady Blanch of Spain, and the Bastard. When the army's drums portend the arrival of the English army, Chatillon ends his report with the advice to prepare either to parley or to fight.

King Philip seems unprepared for the expedition, and so Austria urges the quick preparation of a defense, for which he thinks they are well-prepared. Before either can act, however, King John enters with his parley party to demand surrender from France – or else do battle with England. He declares his action to be justified by an agent of God.

King Philip responds by bidding peace to England, which he claims he loves and represents in the cause of the rightful King of England – Arthur. He cites the natural succession from John's deceased elder brother, Geoffrey, to Geoffrey's son, Arthur. Thus, King Philip concludes that Arthur's cause fits God's plan, *not* John's *unnatural* succession.

King John questions King Philip's right to usurp authority and declare himself to be Arthur's guardian and champion. Eleanor and

Constance then clash. Constance calls John a usurper, and Eleanor calls Arthur a bastard. Constance retorts that Arthur emotionally and physically resembles his father as much as John resembles Eleanor in behavior, and she further implies that *Geoffrey* was more likely to be a bastard, considering the moral consistency of Eleanor. After they mutually criticize each other to the hapless Arthur, Austria calls for quiet, and the Bastard concurs. Austria demands identification of the Bastard, who responds by threatening Austria for his wrongs against Richard, Coeur-de-Lion. Both Blanch and the Bastard refer to Richard's lion's robe, which Austria is wearing.

King Philip impatiently orders the "women and fools" to keep quiet; then he asks King John if John will peacefully relinquish England, Ireland, Angiers, Touraine, and Maine. King John defies France, declaring that he would rather die. Instead, he attempts to seduce Arthur's loyalty with offers of love and rewards. Eleanor urges the boy to come to his grandmother. After Constance caustically comments that if Arthur gives up his kingdom to his grandmother, he will be rewarded with "a plum, a cherry, and a fig." Arthur cries out that he wishes he were dead instead of in the middle of this "coil." Whereupon, Eleanor and Constance castigate each other for shaming the boy. This time, King John demands quiet. Constance adds that Arthur is being punished for Eleanor's sin, and Eleanor retorts that she can produce a will that bars any rights that Arthur might now claim.

Again, King Philip orders the two women to be quiet, and he quickly calls for a summons to the men of Angiers to choose between Arthur and John. A citizen appears and inquires who has summoned him.

King John quickly responds; he says that England calls its "loving subjects"; King Philip interrupts to call them "Arthur's subjects." King John interrupts Philip to point out that French cannons are aimed at the walls of Angiers, and that the British army is there to protect Angiers; therefore, he requests entrance to the city in order to rest. King Philip follows with the reasonable explanation that *he* is there on the behalf of their rightful ruler, Arthur, and he requests only Angiers's acknowledgement of that fact; otherwise, he'll attack.

The citizen of Angiers diplomatically declares that his fellow citizens are loyal subjects of the King of England, but that they have barred their gates until one of the two men proves clear title.

Whereupon, the two kings prepare to battle. The Bastard insults Austria, continuing his own personal vendetta.

Heralds of both kings return to Angiers to report bloody battles and claim victory. The citizen of Angiers observes that the battles have been worthy, but that they did not determine a clear victor as to who could enter the city. The two kings verbally joust about imminent victory.

The Bastard persuades, first, King John, then King Philip, to combine armies against Angiers. His plan is to punish peevish Angiers for defying them, then to battle afterward for the right to rule the conquered city. King John chooses to attack from the West, Austria from the North, and King Philip from the South. The Bastard gleefully realizes that he can manipulate Austria and France into damaging each other by firing artillery into each other's opposite positions.

However, the citizen of Angiers suggests another compromise in order to save his city. Step by step, he leads the kings to consider a match between Lady Blanch of Spain, who is a blood relative of the Coeur-de-Lion, and Lewis, son of the King of France. Blanch's qualities include beauty, virtue, and bloodlines. Each can benefit from the wholeness which marriage provides for them as unfulfilled single people. Furthermore, for the marriage, the gates of Angiers will be unbarred; without it, Angiers will mount a stiff resistance.

The Bastard sullenly mutters that Angiers mounts barrages of words without any force to back their challenge to choose to recognize this proposed marriage or else be prepared to fight a bloody battle. At this point, Eleanor urges King John to grasp this opportunity to prevent King Philip's pursuit of Arthur's cause and thus secure the throne of England.

The citizen of Angiers urges a response from the separately conferring parties. King Philip wants England to speak first because King John had opened the demands for Angiers to choose between them. King John responds by offering a dowry for Lady Blanch "equal with a queen." King Philip then asks Lewis for his reaction. The young prince gazes into Blanch's eyes and declares himself in love.

The Bastard mutters cynicisms about the love match. Lady Blanch promises to do as her uncle wishes and, while stopping short of declarations of love, she does emphasize that she sees nothing in Lewis to hate. After Blanch confirms her willingness to marry, and Lewis confirms his love, King John offers a dowry of the provinces of

Volquessen, Touraine, Maine, Poictiers, and Anjou plus "30,000 marks of English coin" to King Philip. The French king accepts the offer, and the young couple seals the bethrothal with a kiss.

King Philip tells the citizens of Angiers to open their gates for the imminent wedding. He then uneasily asks where Constance is, anticipating her disappointment about the arrangements. He asks King John for advice about how to handle the withdrawal. King John thinks that he can assuage Constance with an offer to elevate Arthur's current title to Duke of Bretagne and Earl of Richmond; then the citizens of Angiers will turn their city over to him. Both kings obviously hope to prevent another tirade from Constance.

The Bastard declares his contempt for the "Mad world! mad Kings! mad composition!" Besides recognizing that King John offered an unnecessary compromise by giving Arthur part of John's kingdom and that King Philip betrayed an honorable cause, the Bastard recognizes that he himself has not benefited from the rules of "commodity" which he has just learned. A fast learner, however, he now pledges his loyalty to the personal benefits which will accompany his commitment to dealing in the rules of trade.

Commentary

Words engulf action in this long, potentially tedious act. Although conflicts seem to abound, the dialogue serves mostly as narrative.

For example, the citizen of Angiers opposes the warring factions and, at one point, he incites the action of battle. However, the battle takes place offstage with its high points narrated for the benefit of the audience; it resolves nothing. That leaves the audience with nothing but the verbal confrontation and, thus, we have little that is dramatic. The Bastard, who agitates for action to settle a conflict, any conflict, aptly summarizes this dialogue between Angiers and the kings when he blurts out: "Here's a large mouth, indeed,/ That spits forth death and mountains, rocks and seas," and he disgustedly summarizes the situation: "Zounds! I was never so bethumped with words/ Since I first called my brother's father dad."

The war of words between Constance and Eleanor is vicious enough to make a boy cry (Arthur) and unsettle two kings, but it does not move the action forward. This is proven by the fact that when the combined efforts of the kings quiet the two women, nothing has changed. The only place in which it is dramatically effective is in

Arthur's case; he is well characterized as a hapless pawn, for he is on-stage and yet separated from all the parleys which will determine his sad fate.

Even the Bastard's conflict with Austria serves only as a belated exposition of the untimely death of Richard the Lion-hearted. This untimely death is verbally structured as being the fulcrum of the unbalancing of the Coeur-de-Lion's succession to power and, thus, the cause of the current conflict between King John and Arthur's supporters.

No single, dominant conflict emerges. Like Act I, this act meanders without a clear focus. Honor, however, appears again as a central factor in characterization. Austria cites his obligation to Arthur, because of his fatal wounding of Richard, albeit in battle, which disrupted the boy's future. Arthur is characterized as being innocent and virtuous. Eleanor and Constance scrap over continence and legitimacy. At the opening of the act, Arthur's allies declaim their "just cause" and vow to fight until they win back Arthur's rights by defeating all the forces that John can muster because of his "unnatural succession." However, by the end of the act, the Bastard shares with us the lessons which he has learned:

> Commodity, the bias of the world;
> The world, who of itself is peised well,
> Made to run even upon even ground,
> Till this advantage, this vile-drawing bias,
> This sway of motion, this Commodity,
> Makes it take head from all indifferency,
> From all direction, purpose, course, intent.

Honor has been engulfed by greed.

The Bastard admits his envy of the kings' lure by "commodity," while he himself has not had the opportunity to choose. As a "beggar," he condemns the vices of the rich, but he looks forward to the time when he can be rich and condemn the vices of beggars. Impressed by the power of "commodity," he vows to worship "gain." The lure of profit is thus added to his original thrill at the sudden power and possession of a title.

In this act, King John succumbs to his flaw—his willful hold on the crown in spite of the legitimate claim of Arthur. Instead of remaining conscientious about his responsibilities, however, he gives away large portions of English territory, hoping to shore up his crumbling powers.

ACT III

Summary

Constance opens the act by summarily rejecting a report of the betrayal of Arthur's cause: "Gone to be married! Gone to swear a peace!/ False blood to false blood joined! Gone to be friends!" She flatly states that she will not accept the hapless messenger's report of the marriage alliance nor the king's gift of provinces since the messenger is a "common man," and she has "a king's oath to the contrary." She threatens the messenger with punishment for alarming her during her vulnerable state. After a series of descriptions of the physical actions of the messenger, who uses body language to support his words, she demands that he speak once more – and then only to confirm the truth of his report.

The messenger, who is Salisbury, does so. Constance, who well understands the implication of destruction, condemns Salisbury for bringing such a message. Salisbury, trapped by the ill fate that comes to the bearer of bad news, tries to separate his report from his responsibility for the events, but Constance refuses to accept that logic.

Arthur begs his mother to "be content." Constance proclaims that if only he had not been so obviously fit to rule, she could be content, but Arthur is in every way so obviously a potential king. She condemns Fortune for whoring with King John and King Philip, and then orders Salisbury to go berate the two kings and tell them they must come to her. Salisbury protests that he cannot approach them unless she accompanies him, but finally he goes, in spite of his doubts.

The kings appear then, accompanied by others in the wedding party. King Philip proclaims the wedding day to be a "blessed day"; Constance contradicts that it is "a wicked day." King Philip protests that she has no cause to complain because he has pledged his "majesty" to her; Constance counters that his majesty is "counterfeit."

Constance indulges in a general expression of outrages which culminates in an insult to Austria. When Austria blusters about what he would do if a *man* said that, the Bastard twice repeats the insult. King John interjects that he disapproves of the Bastard's speaking out of turn.

The entrance of the Pope's legate, Pandulph, interrupts the squabble. He demands to know why King John has interfered with the Pope's appointee as Archbishop of Canterbury. King John responds by denying the power of a mere Pope over the King of England. Speaking for all of England, the King states that "no Italian priest" can usurp a power over English dominion which is held by Heaven alone.

King Philip gasps that this is blasphemy. King John stoutly holds that although all other Christian kings may pay homage to "this meddling priest," *he* opposes the Pope.

Pandulph immediately declares John to be cursed and excommunicated, and he offers blessings to all who revolt against John's rule. He also offers sainthood to anyone who kills John. Constance weaves an alliance with Pandulph, although the Cardinal seems reluctant to admit the similarity of their complaints against King John. Pandulph then orders King Philip to break his alliance with England if John refuses to swear allegiance to Rome. King Philip, for a moment, is unable to act while advice is heaped upon him, with Eleanor, John, and Blanch urging the maintenance of the marital alliance while Austria, Constance, and Lewis urge Philip to forego his pledge to England in order to avoid being cursed as a heretic. King Philip appeals to Pandulph for some gentle compromise to release him from his dilemma, for he is caught between betraying an order of the Pope or betraying the vows of the marriage alliance.

But Pandulph offers no relief. Instead, he demands that King Philip either actively battle England in the name of the Church or expect a curse from the Church. He attacks King Philip's conflict with his conscience by arguing that Philip's vows to the Church take precedence over all other vows. Between Lewis's additional pressure and Pandulph's renewed threat of a curse, Philip succumbs and severs his alliance with England.

After another round of pro and con opinions, France and England prepare to battle. Scene 2 is composed entirely of a brief meeting between King John, Hubert, Arthur, and the Bastard, during which Hubert receives custody of Arthur, and the Bastard assures King John that Eleanor is safe. Scene 3 features a disintegration of the English defenses and of King John's good judgment. King John falsely assures Eleanor that she will be safe if she stays where he is leaving her, and he assures Arthur that *he* will be safe, for he will be under royal protection. King John then dispatches the Bastard to precede them to England, where the Bastard is to amass funds for the war by raiding Church properties. The Bastard declares that "Bell, book, and candle" (excommunication) shall not be a defense against his opportunity to amass valuables and money; then he exits to carry out his assignment.

While Eleanor takes Arthur aside to try to calm him down, King John woos Hubert's loyalty with praise and vague promises in order to persuade him to kill Arthur. All exit then toward their separate destinies – Eleanor to her guarded sanctuary and spy post, Arthur and Hubert to England, and John with the bulk of the army to Calais.

Scene 4 focuses on the gloom of King Philip over France's setbacks. The French armada has been scattered, Angiers lost, Arthur captured, and the English forces have successfully embarked for England after fortifying all captured territories. The French king cannot tolerate either Lewis's assurances that all will eventually go well, nor Constance's remonstrances.

After Constance indulges in grief, Pandulph retorts that she is mad, not grief-stricken. Constance verifies that she *can* distinguish reality, and it is reality that has driven her to consider suicide rather than to exist with her unrelieved grief. King Philip tries to cajole her, then commands her to bind up the hair that she has torn loose. Constance agrees, saying that her hair should not be free while her son is not. She then conjures for Pandulph a scene in which she and Arthur will meet again in heaven, but Arthur will be so disfigured from mistreatment that she will miss the opportunity for reunion because she will not be able to recognize him. Both Pandulph and Philip criticize her fondness for grief. Constance then exits to be alone, and King Philip follows because he fears that she might attempt suicide.

Lewis indulges in melancholy, saying that life is as tedious as a "twice-told tale." Pandulph intrigues him with the prophecy that King John will kill Arthur, which, in turn, will open the way for Lewis and Blanch to claim all that Arthur now holds. Furthermore, they will be supported by all of the English citizens who will rebel because of Arthur's murder. With the additional rebellion which Pandulph predicts will result from the Bastard's ransacking of church property, Lewis is eager to believe the prophecy that a French invasion of England will be joined by a great army of rebels on English soil.

Lewis thus embraces the vision that he will lead this force to a glorious victory and future, and he exits with Pandulph, hoping to convince King Philip to press the invasion of England.

Commentary

Unfortunately, the action halts again in the middle of what has already been a predominantly verbal play. Conceivably, Constance's strident speeches hold the focus, thereby countering the forward movement of the action with her ineffective arguments. She moves the other characters – not to action nor to listening – but into the multi-role of a chorus, telling her to keep quiet.

Rhetoric for and against the marriage obscures the marriage's dramatic significance until Pandulph identifies it for Lewis late in the act. Blanch would be next in line if King John were defeated in battle and if Arthur were killed by his uncle. Because of the power of the male (that will be such an anathema to Queen Elizabeth I), Lewis would then rule England as Blanch's husband.

Another conflict, the religious issue, does move action into a new dimension. When King John refuses to acknowledge the Archbishop of Canterbury, who has ben sent by the Pope, King John takes a stand which was popular with Elizabethan Anglican audiences but which was fatal within the historic context of the play. He defies the conditions which Pandulph offers, and thus he destroys the new alliance and, thereby, he structures the play's dramatic resolution. Pandulph breaks up the alliance by threatening excommunication and a curse for all who align themselves with John. Additionally, he sets up John for murder by declaring sainthood for anyone who can accomplish John's murder. By the end of the act, Pandulph convinces Lewis to invade England. But the focus in this act is blurry because King John is not the prime mover of events, as a protagonist should be. Other than defying Pandulph's commands, making some brief strategic decisions for the war, and planting the seeds for Arthur's accidental death, he does not initiate nor focus the action. As a result, the act moves along awkwardly.

Character development is also weak. Pandulph is a stereotyped, one-dimensional, ambitious Roman Catholic. Constance rants and raves from motivations which are so obscure that other characters in the play express confusion. King Philip wavers, the Bastard declaims, Lewis emotes, Blanch wheedles, Arthur mews, and Austria vegetates. Hubert alone has some moments of depth as he strives to understand and obey his king.

The only full character development occurs within King John. His character and fortune deteriorate when he persuades Hubert to kill Arthur. His assurances to Arthur turn into lies; he dishonors himself by promising protection to Arthur and then arranging the boy's murder. Thus, the King's flaw – the willful capture of the throne – corrupts the patient and wise leadership qualities that he displayed in Act I.

ACT IV

Summary

Hubert orders the executioners, who enter with him, to hide behind the arras until he stamps his foot. Upon hearing the signal, they are to rush out and bind Arthur to a chair. One executioner comments that he hopes Hubert's warrant legitimizes the act. Hubert retorts that the executioner should not voice unacceptable scruples and that he had better obey. The executioners exit then in order to hide.

Arthur enters when he is called by Hubert, and he immediately notices that Hubert appears sad. He says that no one but himself should be sad, and he explains further that he could be happy anywhere but in prison, and that he fears his Uncle John's intentions. He observes that it is not *his* fault that he is Geoffrey's son; he would much rather be Hubert's son so that Hubert would love him.

In an aside, Hubert agonizes over the mercy which is aroused by the boy's conversation. He braces himself to carry out his orders quickly, and even as Arthur expresses his love for Hubert, the burly servant thrusts King John's warrant at Arthur, tells him to read it, and complains in another aside about the tears in his eyes.

Arthur asks: "Must you with hot irons burn out both mine eyes?" Hubert declares that he must, and he will. Arthur reminds his torturer of the time when he bound Hubert's aching head with a princess's handkerchief without ever asking for its return and lovingly tended him throughout the night. Can Hubert remember that night and still blind the eyes that lovingly gazed upon him? Hubert growls that he must do as he promised the king he would. After another appeal for love and mercy from Arthur, Hubert stamps his foot to summon the executioners. Arthur begs Hubert to save him from "these bloody men," and he says that rather than being bound while the executioners blind him, he would rather have Hubert perform the deed. In return, Arthur promises to sit quietly and to forgive Hubert.

Hubert orders the executioners to leave, and one of them expresses relief for being excused from the order. Arthur realizes that he was mistaken when he ordered the compassionate executioner to leave, so he requests his return. Hubert commands the boy to prepare himself.

Instead of keeping his promise to "sit as quiet as a lamb," Arthur incessantly begs Hubert to spare his eyes. The boy gains precious time when the fire needed to re-heat the cold poker goes out, and he calls upon Hubert to show as much mercy as the fire and the irons have.

Finally, Hubert relents and promises to keep the boy safe. Arthur goes to hide, and Hubert exits to spread false stories about Arthur's death, in spite of the danger to himself for having refused a king's command.

In the following scene, King John and some of his advisers examine the current state of affairs. John hopes that his recent second coronation will prove effective. Pembroke remarks that the first should still be in force, but that it was done when there were not symptoms of revolt. Salisbury adds that this second crowning "is wasteful and ridiculous excess." Pembroke and Salisbury comment further that the second coronation might serve only to awaken suspicion about a fault which would not have been noticed previously. Salisbury then oozes flattery for the king by indicating that although King John ignored their advice, they are always pleased to stand by whatever he wants.

King John responds that he shared some of his reasons prior to the coronation and will offer more when his fears have lessened. In the meantime, he is open to all suggestions for reform. Pembroke asks that Arthur be freed on behalf of all those who value the king's safety. The king grants this wish just as Hubert enters.

Pembroke knows that Hubert had a warrant from King John to blind and execute Arthur, and as he observes Hubert's mannerisms during a private conversation with the king, Pembroke believes that the bloody deed is already done. Salisbury also observes that the king shows signs of emotional distress. King John then announces that his desire to free Arthur cannot be carried out because Arthur has just died.

Both Pembroke and Salisbury mutter their fears that stories of the boy's sickness would end this way. King John asks why they frown at him as if he could control life and death. Salisbury blurts that Arthur's death was apparently the result of foul play, and he criticizes the king for it. He and Pembroke exit to find the poor dead child. They predict trouble. King John expresses his regret: "They burn in indignation. I repent."

A messenger enters to report bad news from France. A huge French army has been quickly assembled and dispatched. King John wonders aloud how such an event could escape his mother's knowledge. The messenger then reports that Eleanor died on April 1st and that, according to rumor, Constance also died about three days before that.

King John pleads for time to deal with the loss of his mother, as well as the threat of the gathering French forces, until he can deal with his discontented lords. He is further upset upon learning that Lewis the Dauphin is leading the invasion force.

When the Bastard and Peter of Pomfret enter, the king begs to be spared from more bad news. The Bastard replies that if the king is afraid of "the worst news," then he has none to deliver. King John then composes himself and tells the Bastard to report whatever he wishes to report.

The Bastard says that he was successful in collecting money from Church coffers but, everywhere, he found that people were possessed by unidentifiable fears. He has brought with him the prophet Peter of Pomfret whom he heard predicting that before the next Ascension Day at noon, King John would yield his crown.

King John orders Hubert to imprison the prophet until noon on Ascension Day, when he is to be hanged. Then, Hubert is to return to receive other instructions. After they leave, the king requests any news that the Bastard may have about the French army. The Bastard says that everyone is talking about the landing of the army. Furthermore, he himself met up with an agitated group led by Bigot and Salisbury, who were searching for Arthur's body.

The king requests that the Bastard find the group and persuade them to come to him so that they can be persuaded to love him again. The Bastard says that he will. King John urges him to hurry, because he cannot afford a domestic rebellion when a foreign army is invading. King John then sends the messenger after the Bastard in case messages need to be relayed; afterward, he grieves: "My mother dead!"

Hubert enters to report a natural phenomenon – four fixed moons with a fifth in "wondrous motion." People were awed by the sight and have begun to whisper about Arthur's death. The king is furious at the reminder of the people's fears and Arthur's death. He complains, "Thy hand hath murdered him. I had a mighty cause/ To wish him dead, but thou hadst none to kill him."

Hubert protests that he merely followed orders. King John implies that Hubert *misunderstood* their conversation and acted without authority upon that misunderstanding. When Hubert produces the signed warrant, King John wriggles away from responsibility for the evidence. Instead, he blames Hubert for being there, for looking like a killer, and thus inspiring him to think about the warrant. Hubert, he says, should have employed his conscience and resisted the order instead of turning the king's moment of weakness into a bloody deed. Furthermore, John says that a simple pause at the time he issued the warrant would have been enough resistance to stop him.

Since Hubert made the mistake of carrying out a flawed command, King John dismisses him with the warning to stay out of his sight forever. The king recognizes that his order to kill Arthur has resulted in "civil tumult" just when he needs a kingdom united against the French invasion.

Hubert then assures King John that he can arm the country against the invaders, because Arthur is alive. He also complains that the king has misjudged by equating the quality of his conscience with his physical appearance. King John urges Hubert to go and report Arthur's survival to the angry lords, and then he apologizes for his angry criticisms of Hubert's rough looks.

In Scene 3, Arthur counters all efforts to save his life. While poised on the high prison walls, disguised as a ship-boy, Arthur begs the ground below not to hurt him when he jumps. He conjectures that if he does not break any bones, he has many alternatives for his escape; if he dies, he believes that such a fate will be preferable to staying in prison. The jump is fatal.

Arthur dies just as the search party appears. Salisbury, Pembroke, and Bigot decide to accept an invitation to a meeting with Pandulph the next morning. At this point, the Bastard enters to deliver King John's request for an immediate meeting.

Salisbury composes a message for the Bastard to deliver: they will not serve a king with such a stained reputation. The Bastard cautions whatever their thoughts, the lords should use "good words." Salisbury retorts that they are now ruled by grief, not good manners.

Just as the Bastard leads up to the good news that Arthur is alive, they discover the boy's body. Salisbury declares Arthur's murder to be the vilest in history. Pembroke extends this comparison into the future as a murder heinous enough to minimize all murders yet uncommitted. The Bastard agrees it is damnable "if that it be the work of any hand." Salisbury dismisses the "if" and blames King John and Hubert, then vows dedication of his life to revenge. Pembroke and Bigot concur with the vow.

Hubert suddenly bursts in to joyously announce that Arthur is alive. Salisbury draws his sword to convince Hubert to get out of their sight. A confused Hubert states that he will defend himself even against a lord of the realm. Bigot and Pembroke join the threats against Hubert; the Bastard urges them to "keep the peace." Salisbury and the Bastard then threaten each other with death. Hubert explains that he loved the boy, left him alive an hour before, and he joins them in their mourning.

Salisbury warns his group not to be deceived by Hubert's cunning tears, and he calls for all who abhor such slaughter as what happened to Arthur to leave with him. Bigot and Pembroke announce that they will leave for a meeting with the Dauphin at Bury; King John can find them there.

The Bastard then states how damned Hubert is—if he so much as "agreed" to this vile murder—and he states further that he suspects that Hubert *was* involved. Once again, Hubert cannot utter a convincing word in his own defense. Finally, he declares that if he in any way contributed to the boy's death, hell can inflict its worst tortures, but "I left him well."

As ordered, Hubert picks up Arthur's body to carry it away for burial. The Bastard declares his amazement at "how easy thou dost take all England up!" With a clear vision of the turmoil that now threatens England, the Bastard leaves to join the king.

Commentary

Action finally moves forward with sudden dramatic focus in Act IV, although the action here, as in the previous acts, is composed of actions which seem complex. All events here center around John's willful hold on the throne.

As an example of improved dramatic focus, the conflict between King John and Arthur is better represented than earlier. Pembroke and Salisbury are more emotionally involved in Arthur's cause than were France and Austria, so they project more emotional tension to the audience. They are also more effective. Furthermore, the threat of civil revolt because of Arthur's death was an emotionally arousing theme for Shakespeare's contemporaries—even more arousing and fearful than a foreign invasion.

Obviously, the conflict between John and Arthur also becomes direct. The king orders the boy to be killed; the boy dissuades the executioners. On the other hand, when King John wants Arthur to live, the boy ironically thwarts the king's wish by his fatal, desperate leap for freedom.

France is still threatening to invade England, as it was when Act I opened, but by being separated from Arthur's cause, France is clearly defined as an enemy. The audience can now focus its sympathies against France and *for* England. France takes on a hateful image, a ghoul preying on reactions to Arthur's death.

Unfortunately, action is still sometimes heated because of excessive verbiage. For example, the dramatic action of a swordfight between Hubert and Salisbury bogs down in speeches such as Hubert's

> Stand back, Lord Salisbury, stand back, I say!
> By heaven, I think my sword's as sharp as yours.
> I would not have you, lord, forget yourself,
> Nor tempt the danger of my true defense,
> Lest I, by marking of your rage, forget
> Your worth, your greatness, and nobility.
>
> (IV.iii.80-85)

And all of Arthur's lengthy appeals to spare his sight and life are almost melodramatically sentimental:

> O heaven, that there were but a mote in your [eyes],
> A grain, a dust, a gnat, a wandering hair,
> Any annoyance in that precious sense.
> Then feeling what small things are boisterous there,
> Your vile intent must needs seem horrible.
>
> (IV.iii.92-96)

However, two major structural flaws also diminish tension and continuity of action. First, the conflict between King John against the Pope, a popular stand for contemporaries of Shakespeare, is not continued from the previous act. Thus, an important link is missing. Second, this act features no human protagonist. Events turn and twist both King John and Arthur — the two featured characters, and although one could argue that England is the protagonist, the argument does not hold up well for the entire act.

If anything, the action in Act IV develops a convoluted philosophy about King John's flaw — his willful hold on the throne. His fearful second coronation arouses suspicions about his right to the throne. Although Shakespeare's contemporaries were aware that the Yorks employed suspicious means to gain and hold the throne of England, they did not believe that mere suspicions or disagreement justified civil rebellion. Rather, measured against a world order in which the kingship was established by God, people believed that no one had the right to overthrow the king unless that king were to issue an order that would demand that the citizens disobey one of God's commandments. Thereby hangs the significance of much of what is said and done in this act. King John's order for Hubert to kill Arthur is judged as heinous murder. Had King John's order been obeyed, the king would have been culpable, and the rebels would have acted correctly. However, since King John is guilty *only of the thought*, and Arthur kills himself by his own foolish, desperate decision, the rebels are wrong. Hubert and the Bastard take actions which are correct for the sake of world order and England.

The Bastard's final line in this act, however, identifies the issue as unresolved: "And heaven itself doth frown upon the land." And subsequent civil war upholds the opinion that England is not operating in a manner which is acceptable to Heaven. This play's historical context represents fearful memories of the thirteenth-century civil war and the subsequent years of instability, which were caused by the conflicts of the Yorks vs. the Lancasters. The Tudor line was regarded as a safeguard against civil war, and Queen Elizabeth I is remembered for her obsession with peace.

All of these fears emerge in one of the Bastard's speeches — the fear of chaos that follows civil war, the disruption of the chain of being because a young boy is dead:

I am amazed, methinks, and lose my way
Among the thorns and dangers of this world.

* * * * * * * * * * * * * * * * *

Now for the bare-picked bone of majesty
Doth doggèd war bristle his angry crest
And snarleth in the gentle eyes of peace.
Now powers from home and discontents at home
Meet in one line, and vast confusion waits,
As doth a raven on a sick-fallen beast,
The imminent decay of wrested pomp.
Now happy he whose cloak and cincture can
Hold out this tempest.

(IV.iv.139-156)

Hubert successfully fends off all who would stereotype him as a two-dimensional character who looks like and, therefore, is a murderer. His sense of honor emerges in the form of integrity, a quality of which Hubert is proud. In fact, his sense of honor and conscience respond to Arthur's appeals for mercy, which, in turn, creates an inner conflict and eventually overwhelms the order of a king. Thus, Hubert becomes a three-dimensional character during this act.

The Bastard continues to develop. In each previous act, he learned and shared one important lesson. Act IV is no exception. Here, he learns how fearful are disloyalty and disrespect (aspects of honor) that are channeled into civil rebellion. Unlike the bold embracing of new concepts which the Bastard exhibited previously, a cold flailing against an unacceptable lesson emerges when he says, "I am amazed . . . and lose my way." Thus, fear and doubt add another layer to the Bastard's character. With loyalty stretched almost to the breaking point by Arthur's death, the Bastard chooses to support King John for the sake of stability, exhibiting again the quality of honor which, although much shallower before, marked him from his first appearance. The Bastard is now the most fully developed character in the play.

King John does not fare as well. Instead of developing the wise and patient leadership qualities that he exhibited in Act I, he is now deteriorating. His flaw now dominates every action, and it appears to be toppling him from the height of his monarchy. Although still patriotic to the extent that he wants to defend England against

foreign invaders, he is no longer conscientious about his responsibilities. He does realize that he has contributed to a disastrous civil
tumult. And he refuses to accept responsibility for the death of Arthur. Instead, he blames Hubert, claiming that had Hubert but
hesitated, the order would not have been signed. John's moral
disintegration has diminished him to a shadow, a character who in-
teracts with no one. His role is reduced to a symbol needed for national security.

ACT V

Summary

King John enters into a ceremony of contrition with Pandulph.
Having handed over his crown to Pandulph, John receives it again
with the blessings of the Pope. In return, Pandulph promises to stop
the war that he began. Pandulph marks the day of conversion as
Ascension Day. After Pandulph leaves, King John remembers the
prophecy and expresses relief that yielding his crown before noon
was a voluntary act.

The Bastard brings bad news again: Kent has surrendered; London has welcomed the Dauphin and his troops; most of the English
lords have joined the French forces. King John asks why the lords
did not return to his service after they had learned that Arthur was
alive. The Bastard tells the king of their discovery of Arthur's body.
Upon learning that Hubert was mistaken about Arthur's survival, the
king is overcome by despair. The Bastard then urges his king to display
courage, to challenge his enemies, and to lead his remaining supporters
to an attack.

King John announces the agreement which he arranged with the
Pope's legate. The Bastard remonstrates his king for this "inglorious"
compromise; he disapproves of arranging a truce with the invaders,
and he takes special exception to yielding to the arrogant young
Dauphin. Again, the Bastard urges a brave defense, if for no other
reason, than to act as insurance in case Pandulph cannot deliver the
promised peace.

King John assigns the fight to the Bastard's leadership. They leave
as the Bastard exhorts his king to meet the odds with courage.

Scene 2 features the Dauphin and his followers. Lewis dictates to Count Melun the oaths sworn by the rebel English lords. Salisbury affirms his allegiance but regrets that he must kill his countrymen. He bewails the sickness within his government that has driven him to heal it by joining forces with invaders of his homeland, then excuses himself to weep.

Lewis praises Salisbury for both his decision and the war of conscience that he is fighting. The Dauphin declares that even he himself is moved by Salisbury's manly tears. He urges Salisbury to compose himself, to fight, and to look forward to the rewards. Seeing Pandulph, Lewis anticipates a blessing on their enterprise.

Instead, Pandulph announces King John's reconciliation with the Pope as a cause for withdrawing the French attack. Lewis responds that he is too proud and "high-born" to be controlled by the commands of a secondary power. He says that Pandulph's voice kindled the war but that Pandulph is too weak to blow out the resulting flames. Lewis claims that John's peace with Rome has nothing to do with peace with France. Furthermore, the Dauphin claims England because of his marriage to Blanch. He wants to press the battles that have nearly guaranteed the prize. He denies that Rome has any jurisdiction over this campaign. Pandulph says that Lewis is considering only externals in this issue. Lewis declares that he will not return until he wins this war.

At this unfavorable moment, the Bastard arrives to inquire about the progress of the negotiations. Pandulph reports on the Dauphin's refusal to stop the war. The Bastard hurls brave challenges at both the Dauphin and the English rebels, painting a portrait of a brave King John who stands ready to lead his loyal countrymen in a successful defense.

Lewis dismisses both the Bastard and Pandulph, refusing to listen any more. He announces that war will win his arguments. The Bastard warns the Dauphin that his drums announce the beginning of the battles that will defeat the invaders.

Scene 3 consists of bad news for the British. Hubert informs King John that their forces are faring badly in the day's battles. King John informs Hubert that he feels ill. A messenger informs the king that the Bastard wants him to leave the battlefield. King John informs everyone that he is withdrawing to go to the abbey at Swinstead; he bemoans the fact that his fever prevents him from celebrating the news that the French supply armada was wrecked at sea, and he orders a litter to carry him away.

In Scene 4, the rebel English lords worry about their setbacks. Salisbury expresses surprise at the number of supporters of King John, Pembroke urges vigorous support for the French or they themselves will lose, and Bigot blames the Bastard for the astonishing defense.

A mortally wounded Count Melun manages to reach the group and urges them to join other English lords who have abandoned their cause in order to re-pledge loyalty to King John, because Lewis had pledged to behead any rebels upon the moment of his victory. When the lords express doubt, Count Melun assures them that he tells the truth because he is dying and because his grandfather was English. In return, Melun requests help to assist him to a quiet place to die. The English lords agree both to help Melun and to rush back to King John.

In Scene 5, Lewis must cope with bad news about Count Melun's death, the English lords' defection, and the armada's destruction.

In the next scene, through a series of codes which lead one to believe that they cannot see each other in the black night, Hubert and the Bastard meet. Their exchange of news is also bleak. Hubert reports that the king has been poisoned, apparently by a monk, but has a slight chance of recovering. The good news is that all of the English lords have returned and been pardoned at Prince Henry's request. The Bastard, in turn, reports that half his fighting forces have been lost to a sudden, devastating turn in the battle. Having barely escaped on his fast horse, he asks Hubert to lead him to the king.

In the seventh and final scene, Prince Henry appears and takes charge. He reports that King John is dying. Pembroke adds that the king believes that he can recover if he is brought into the fresh air; he is more patient now and has been singing. When Prince Henry bemoans death's deterioration of his father's body and mind, Salisbury assures him that Henry is well suited to fit the vacant throne.

King John is carried in. He praises the comfort of the open air for his fever and pain. He tells Prince Henry that he, John has been poisoned, and he blames all around him for not supplying cold air to help him. Prince Henry offers his tears, but they are rejected as too hot and salty.

The king clings to a thread of life until the Bastard can deliver his news. This news is that the Dauphin is advancing against defense forces that were devastated by the unexpected turn in the battle. King John dies.

Salisbury urges Prince Henry to take over the monarchy. The prince is unnerved by his father's "demonstration of mortality." The Bastard appeals to Heaven to aid him in revenging the king's death, after which he pledges continued servitude after death.

Salisbury says that Pandulph awaits within for acceptance of a tolerable offer of peace. The Bastard urges a strong defense first. But Salisbury convinces the Bastard that nothing else is necessary because the Dauphin has already prepared for the ceremony.

Commentary

Unfortunately, Act V does not maintain Act IV's improved focus. There is, however, a focal point – King John's deterioration and death occupy our thoughts. But that focus is not dramatic, because it is not the center of conflicts and tension. John, leader of England, is no longer opposing the rebellion. Instead, he assigns England's defense to the Bastard and withdraws eventually to Swinstead Abbey. After Salisbury's demonstration of ambiguity, all of the rebels return to the fold and sheepishly await the death of the man whom they swore to destroy. But they do not act as a result of any action that King John initiates, and so this entire conflict recedes in dramatic impact.

When word of France's peace offer arrives, no one even verifies the terms; they just grab what they can get. And this peace offer leaves a question: why did the Dauphin give up the fight? After jeopardizing his immortal soul in a confrontation with Pandulph, Lewis reappears in one brief scene to hear some bad news. The next thing we know, he has given up – even though the Bastard dropped his defense.

In addition, the role of Pandulph deteriorates. We are left wondering whether or not he actually convinced Lewis to negotiate the peace (which would answer the question of why Lewis gave up), or whether he has been reduced to a role of an emissary. Either way, Shakespeare fails to justify Pandulph's actions; Shakespeare thus withholds a potentially important dramatic change from the audience.

That failure, plus the failure to resolve the end of the rebellion through dramatic conflict, are key weaknesses in this play. It is doubtful that anyone deeply cares when John, who is intended to be the central character in this play, faces failure and dies. His deterioration and death, the reuniting of England under Prince Henry, and the withdrawal of the French forces are merely catalogued in a series of narrative speeches. John's death serves as the playwright's need to resolve all of the issues and to set up Prince Henry as a reconciliation figure in order to end this play.

Because Shakespeare wrote a weak, forced conclusion which does not grow naturally out of events which preceded it, he could do little more than provide his characters with declamatory speeches.

Characterization fares little better than plot in Act V. As mentioned in the preceding summary, characters do not interact in order to develop conflict; they declaim. Prince Henry arouses curiosity, but he is a wooden figure without personality. Identified as the son of King John and as the only hope for England's unity, he nevertheless remains a dull character when he should be arousing hope and inspiring cheers.

Even the Bastard departs from the pattern of learning one important lesson per act. Here, he serves only to lead an unsuccessful defense and to deliver bad news. He is devastated when he is told to accept the peace.

One interpretation of this ending which can structure unity is that, in the end, everyone must capitulate to political reality—the merciless, unyielding "policy" which overrules humanistic, passionate objections. Constance rebelled against the system but hers was a hopeless, uncompromising protest which resulted in a frenzied death. In contrast, once the Bastard accepts the fact that the system is corrupt and accomodates himself to that fact, he gains power. Once he comes to terms with political realities, he accepts without protest the French terms of peace, King John's death, and the need to prepare Prince Henry to take over the government. The spirited protester at Angiers is as dead as the illegitimate king.

That interpretation notwithstanding, plot and characterization, both of which displayed intermittent promise during the development of the play, diminish toward the conclusion of *King John*. Perhaps it was enough for Elizabethan audiences to witness the reuniting of England and the defeat of the French, but those events are not, in themselves, sufficient to stir modern audiences to cheers or catharsis at the climax of this play.

QUESTIONS FOR REVIEW

1. List some of the favorable qualities of King John as they are dramatized in Act I.

2. Identify a major conflict within King John. Is this conflict resolved?

3. Is the seige of Angiers a probable series of events?

4. Describe how unity is (or is not) achieved through the religious issue.

5. Identify the motivation for Constance's actions.

6. What is the significance of the marriage between Blanch and Lewis at its inception? Later?

7. Does John have any right to be king? Why or why not?

8. Describe the character of the Bastard.

9. Comment on the effects of the death of Arthur.

10. Why won't people believe Hubert when he tells them that Arthur is alive?

11. What is the role of Pandulph in the development of action?

12. What significant historical events are dramatized in this play?

13. Does the Bastard ever apply the lessons about Commodity that he learned?

14. Does Arthur best exemplify Elizabethan melancholy or Senecan stoicism?

15. Name the characters, if any, who were adequately motivated and consistent.

SELECTED BIBLIOGRAPHY

ADAMS, J. Q. *A Life of William Shakespeare.* Boston: Houghton Mifflin Co., 1923.

ALLEN, RALPH G. and JOHN GASSNER, ed. *Theatre and Drama.* 2 vols. Boston: n.p., 1964.

BENTLEY, GERALD E. *Shakespeare: A Bibliographical Handbook.* New Haven: Yale University Press, 1961.

BOWERS, FREDSON T. *Elizabethan Revenge Tragedy.* Magnolia, MA: Peter Smith, 1958.

BRADBROOK, M. C. *Themes and Conventions of Elizabethan Tragedy.* 2nd ed. Cambridge: Cambridge University Press, 1980.

BRADLEY, A. C. *Shakespearean Tragedy.* London: The Macmillan Co., 1904.

CALDERWOOD, JAMES C. "Commodity and Honor in *King John.*" *University of Toronto Quarterly,* XXIX (1960), 341-56.

CAMPBELL, LILY. *Shakespeare's "Histories": Mirrors of Elizabethan Policy.* San Marino, CA: Huntington Library, 1978.

CHAMBERS, E. K. *William Shakespeare.* New York: Oxford University Press, 1930.

CREIZENACH, WILHELM. *The English Drama in the Age of Shakespeare.* Reprint of 1916 edition. Boston: Dynamic Learn Corp., 1979.

DAVIS, JOYCE O., ed. *King John & Matilda: A Critical Edition.* Renaissance Drama Series. New York: Garland Publishers, 1980.

DRIVER, T. F. *The Sense of History in Greek and Shakespearean Drama.* New York: Columbia University Press, 1960.

ELLIS-FERMORE, UNA. *Shakespeare the Dramatist and Other Papers*, ed. Kenneth Muir. New York: Barnes & Noble, Inc., 1961.

ELSON, JOHN. "Studies in the *King John* Plays." *Joseph Quincy Adams Memorial Studies.* Washington, D.C.: Folger Shakespeare Library, 1948.

GRANVILLE-BARKER, HARLEY. *Prefaces to Shakespeare*, 4th series. London: Sidgewick and Jackson, Ltd., 1945.

HARRISON, G. B. *Shakespeare's Tragedies.* Oxford University Press, 1951.

HONIGMANN, E. A. J., ed. *Shakespeare's* King John. New Arden edition. Cambridge, Mass.: Harvard University Press, 1969.

JOSEPH, BERTRAM. *Acting Shakespeare.* New York: Theatre Arts, 1969.

KOKERITZ, HELGE. *Shakespeare's Names: A Pronouncing Dictionary.* New Haven: Yale University Press, 1959.

PARROTT, THOMAS MARC and ROBERT HAMILTON BALL. *A Short View of Elizabethan Drama.* New York: Charles Scribner's Sons, 1958.

PRICE, H. T. "Construction in *Titus Andronicus*," *Shakespeare: The Tragedies, A Collection of Critical Essays*, ed. Alfred Harbage. New Jersey: Prentice-Hall, Inc., 1964.

PRICE, J. R. "*King John* and the Problematic Art," *Shakespeare Quarterly*, XXI (1970), 25-28.

RIBNER, IRVING. *The English History Play in the Age of Shakespeare.* New York: Octagon, 1979 Reprint of 1957 edition.

WILSON, J. D., ed. *Shakespeare's* King John. Cambridge: University Press, 1954.

TILLYARD, E. M. W. *The Elizabethan World Picture.* New York: Vintage Books, n.d.

NOTES

NOTES

NOTES

NOTES